AVOID THEM LIKE THE PLAGUE

AVOID THEM LIKE THE PLAGUE

A BOOK OF CLICHÉS

NIGEL FOUNTAIN

Michael O'Mara Books Limited

This paperback edition first published in 2015

First published in hardback under the title *Clichés: Avoid Them Like the Plague!* in Great Britain in 2012 by

Michael O'Mara Books Limited
9 Lion Yard
Tremadoc Road
London SW4 7NQ

A CIP catalogue record for this book is available from the British Library.

Papers used by Michael O'Mara Books Limited are natural, recyclable products made from wood grown in sustainable forests. The manufacturing processes conform to the environmental regulations of the country of origin.

ISBN: 978-1-78243-428-3 in paperback print format
ISBN: 978-1-84317-796-8 in EPub format
ISBN: 978-1-84317-797-5 in Mobipocket format

1 2 3 4 5 6 7 8 9 10

www.mombooks.com

Designed and typeset by www.glensaville.com
Cover design by Lucy Stephens

Printed and bound by CPI Group (UK) Ltd, Croydon, CR0 4YY

Contents

INTRODUCTION

'In the beginning,' Saint John tells us in his Gospel, 'was the word.' Soon after, as he keeps quiet about, came the cliché. There are ancient clichés, lovingly handed down from generation unto generation; there are old, half-timbered clichés, with roots in Elizabethan England and, once the Industrial Revolution got going, clichés that put their coats on and got going too. Modern clichés, meanwhile, can graze on the rich and verdant pasturelands (adding adjectives always helps) of Hollywood, the Internet, television, and pop.

The King James Bible, that literary classic, has provided a bottomless pit of source material for older clichés. So too have William Shakespeare, John Milton and Charles Dickens. These are class acts! So what is going on? Their observations were dazzling insights, new ways of seeing the world. Then someone else said them. And someone else repeated them, and eventually someone said, 'Look, I know this is a cliché, but all the same . . . '

The word cliché has its origins in mid-nineteenth-century France, and refers, as the *Oxford English Dictionary* (*OED*) puts it, to a 'metal stereotype or electrotype block' used in printing. Hence 'a stereotyped expression, a hackneyed phrase or opinion'. The hackney horse was often kept for hire, as was the hackney carriage, and thus an unoriginal phrase becomes hackneyed, tired, overused – a cliché.

Compiling this book, I was drawn (like a moth to a flame) towards advertising, 'celebrity culture' and politics. But then, these areas provide such splendid nesting grounds for clichés. Practitioners in such trades are so often engaged in the creation of mass moods, and herd instincts, a climate (cliché-sphere?) where 'movers and shakers', 'right-thinking people' and 'A-list celebs' can run wild, run free, amid 'blue-sky thinking'.

All right, you say, we may profess to despise clichés, yet they are part of how we communicate. Indeed. But recognize them for what they are. Consider replacing them with bright, shining new thoughts, tiring perhaps - rewarding certainly. Every man and woman a Shakespeare, a Jane Austen, a Bob Dylan, a Lady Gaga!

The worst class of clichés, meanwhile, will continue to stagger towards us, like the *Night of the Living Dead* crowd, getting up when knocked down, looking in the window, scratching at the door, moving in, making themselves a snack, taking up residence. And the borderlines between zombie phrases and the rest are indeed disputed territory, and one person's cliché may be a respectable catchphrase, idiom or proverb to someone else. But clichés, adept at sneaking into the language, once identified, turn themselves in (and then make a break for it). Where thought should be provoked, there is repetition, the confirmation of the mundane, the expected, the banal.

Time, like an ever-rolling stream, bears some clichés

away. How many people now use 'castles in Spain', which Eric Partridge in his *Dictionary of Clichés* (1940) described as 'fond imagining'? Or 'sitting at the receipt of custom' (sitting at the cash desk)? Indeed, both are rather elegant phrases when compared, for instance, with 'bottom lines' and 'ballpark figures'.

Other clichés have extraordinary longevity. It was a surprise to me to find that 'square the circle', which I, in my naivety, had imagined was a peculiarly irritating phrase from the latter part of the twentieth century, has a history that dates back to the early seventeenth. And it was a surprise as well to find that the term 'politically correct', from which comes the cliché 'political correctness gone mad', has its origins in late-eighteenth-century America, far earlier than most people imagine, for the beginning of its ascent to cliché-dom was in the 1950s. Even so, antiquity is not necessarily a reason to prolong the overuse of such constructions in everyday language . . .

NIGEL FOUNTAIN

Affluent Society

Famous at Harvard and Princeton Universities, and perhaps the closest thing in his era to being America's leading public intellectual, the Canadian-born economist John Kenneth Galbraith published *The Affluent Society* in 1958. The book, described by *The New York Times* as 'A compelling challenge to conventional thought', was a bestseller (and remains in print), the phrase went into the language, but, along a trajectory through time, its meaning was transformed. Galbraith's purpose had been to emphasize the gap between private affluence and public poverty, and the need for more equitable policies. He died in 2006, having lived to see greater affluence, a growing gap between rich and poor, and half the time his term used as a celebration, not a condemnation, one online dictionary even defining it as 'a society in which the material benefits of prosperity are widely available', which is not at all what Galbraith had meant. It has become a cliché through lazy use of the phrase to mean established and increasing prosperity, rather than the ever-widening gulf between the haves and have-nots.

A-LIST CELEB

And there are Bs, Cs and downwards to Zs. As *Closer* – a British magazine celebrating people's ability to be photographed while moving between nightclubs and film premières – explains, 'every A-lister's nightmare' may well include proximity to those lower down the alphabetical listing of celeb-ness. 'Celeb', an abbreviation of 'celebrity', is American and, surprisingly, dates from the early twentieth century, the first record in print appearing in a Lincoln, Nebraska, daily newspaper in 1913. 'A-list', in the sense, as the *Oxford English Dictionary* (*OED*) puts it, of 'a social, professional, or celebrity elite', is also American in origin and dates from the 1930s. Some people are always fighting their way around the alphabet and wanting to be let in. During New York's late-nineteenth-century 'Gilded Age', 'Mrs

Astor's Four Hundred' were those people whom the society hostess deemed suitable to grace her ballroom, which did not include the 'New Rich' or (well-bred shudder!) arrivistes. But Mrs A. did not have tabloid newspapers and celebrity (read 'gossip') magazines to contend – or sign contracts – with. Factory-farmed celebs date from the 1980s, and, like Oscar Wilde's cynic, know 'the price of everything and the value of nothing'. The phrase is thoroughly overworked; besides, while 'A-list celeb' is generally used approvingly, anything from B down is invariably pejorative.

ALL THE BELLS AND WHISTLES

A phrase meaning all the attractive, but not essential, additional extras or accessories, and, in computing, particularly, 'speciously attractive but superfluous facilities'. It is thought to be a reference to a fairground organ, those large steam-driven contraptions designed to produce loud music above the sound of the crowd and the machinery of the fair. Quite apart from the organ pipes, these had all sorts of extras such as cymbals, whistles, drums and so on, rather like a giant mechanical one-man band. The expression seems to have been in use from the late 1960s

– one source quotes an advertisement for a used car in a Wisconsin newspaper, *The Capital Times*, in June 1971 – and to have become established in computing by the late 1970s, the *OED* citing a US magazine, *Byte*, which in July 1977 referred to 'outputs that can be used to provide user-defined functions, such as enabling external devices or turning on bells and whistles'. From there it moved into commerce – applied, for instance, to the optional extras on a new car – and crossed into journalism and general business, referring increasingly to less tangible accessories, as in this, from *Financial Executive* magazine of May 2010: 'One would think that most chief financial officers, tax executives and business owners take full advantage of all the bells and whistles provided in the United States tax code.' The upshot is that the phrase is now mainly used as another way of saying that something is loaded with features, without necessarily any implication that while these may be appealing, they are unnecessary or even pointless. Just as fairground organs were phased out from the 1920s when reliable public loudspeaker systems came in, this expression has probably exceeded its usefulness.

ALL (OTHER) THINGS BEING EQUAL

This phrase, from the Latin *ceteris paribus* meaning 'with other things the same', has been in use since the seventeenth century, and was once generally applied to mathematics or the sciences, where measurements have to be precise. The English translation first appeared in print in Macaulay's *History of England* (1849), and in 1889 the *Saturday Review* probably failed to allay the fears of soldiers and their families with this effort: 'Other things being equal, the chances of any man being hit in action vary . . . with the rate of fire to which he is exposed.' As the meaning lost some precision, so it could be applied to more aspects of life – 'Languages are an asset in many careers, and other things being equal, the candidate who can offer languages may get the job,' *The Sunday Times* told us in 2004; while in a February 2012 article in *The Washington Times* discussing the president's defence policy, we read of 'the Middle East, North Africa and beyond. All other things being equal, "beyond" may include: the Far East . . . China and North Korea . . . Russia . . .' But by this time the phrase had already become a cliché, meaning little more than 'if conditions stay the way they are now; if nothing happens to complicate things,' and indeed used simply to pad a statement. 'All things being equal, I should arrive about ten o'clock' means exactly the same as 'I should arrive about ten o'clock.'

American as apple pie, As

In *Catch-22*, that unsurpassed satire of military service in the Second World War, Joseph Heller wrote of what drove the boys to lay down their lives: 'The hot dog, the Brooklyn Dodgers, Mom's apple pie. That's what everyone's fighting for.' In short, it was an issue of pies and patriotism, though the exact pie content is up for grabs. Blueberry pie is sometimes mentioned (it is, after all, the official dessert of the State of Maine), while journalists have asserted over the years that pizza (originating as pie Naples-style) is 'as American as apple pie', as are Marilyn, Elvis, Chevys (especially those in Don McLean's 1970s hit song called, uh, 'American Pie'), the Yankees and Miley Cyrus. H. Rap Brown (or Jamil Abdullah al-Amin), once a leading figure in the Black Panther Party, famously added to the discussion in the 1960s by proclaiming that 'violence is as American as cherry pie', which rather dispels the aura of Norman Rockwell-like wholesome home baking. Sometimes, too, the line blurs. The Super Bowl is definitely as apple pie as it comes, but Janet Jackson exposing a breast live on TV during the halftime entertainment for Super Bowl XXXVIII in Houston, Texas, is not. The phrase, which seems first to have appeared in print in an advertisement in the *Gettysburg Times* in 1924, is thoroughly worn out: if the American writer and documentary maker Martin Torgoff can write 'Drugs have become as American as apple pie,' it is probably time to find a new expression to describe the nation's typical and traditional virtues. *See also* **Catch–22**.

AT THE END OF THE DAY

. . . comes the night?
. . . the sun sets?
. . . we all go home?
. . . we go to a bar?

This monstrously overworked phrase could mean all of these, and many more, but it doesn't. Indeed, most of the time it is a phrase churned out because the churner-out can't think of anything else to say – so it often means 'When everything else has been said on the matter.' Or it could mean 'ultimately', or even 'most important'. It is lazy and long-winded; no wonder it has been voted 'most hated cliché' – though this has not prevented its continuing overuse . . . It is defined by the *OED* as a 'hackneyed phrase' meaning 'eventually' or 'when all's said and done' (the latter another hackneyed phrase), and its first recorded appearance in print in this usage seems to date from 1974. *See also* **At this moment in time**.

AT THIS MOMENT IN TIME

The *OED* gives the main meaning of 'moment' as 'a portion of time too brief for its duration to be taken into account'; America's equally revered *Merriam-Webster's Dictionary* (*Webster's*) similarly defines it as 'a comparatively brief period of time'. So what this most hated and hackneyed phrase means is 'a time in time'. The earliest examples in print of the phrase in the UK were in a 1972 novel and in *The Guardian* of 12 March 1973: 'The usual stuff about meaningful confrontations taking place. . . at this moment in time.' It seems to have come into the English language at about the time another phrase was in circulation, 'at this point in time', which *The Columbia Guide to Standard American English* (1993) described as 'a bit of padded prose', explaining that 'the Watergate hearings of the 1970s made many people conscious of it and determined to root it out of their language.' Thus a piece of overused padding was replaced by a piece of meaningless – and now also overused – padding. Why not the clear and succinct 'now', or even 'at the moment'?

AVOID IT (THEM, HIM *ETC.*) LIKE THE PLAGUE!

There is much to be avoided like the plague. Internet scams, overly popular holiday destinations, trans-fats, factory-farmed chickens, virus e-mails, to name but a few. If you're a millionaire sportsman, you can add busty girls in nightclubs who want to sleep with you so they can sell a story to the press. (Millionaire sportsmen can be slow to pick up on that kind of thing.) There are certainly good reasons to avoid the plague. Daniel Defoe's *A Journal of the Plague Year* (1722) describes the outbreak of bubonic plague in London, 1665: 'The swellings, which were generally in the neck and groin, when they grew hard, and would not break, grew so painful, that it was equal to the most exquisite torture; and some, not able to bear the torment, threw themselves out at windows, or shot themselves, or otherwise made themselves away.' The phrase itself was already well established by the time of the 1918–19 Spanish flu pandemic, which is thought to have killed between 50 and 100 million of the world's population, accounting for more than half of America's military deaths in the First World War. Twelve years after the end of that war a group of Chicago businessmen calling themselves 'The Secret Six' said they aimed to make the Windy City a place mobsters, and especially Al Capone, would indeed 'avoid like the plague', an endeavour in which they met with some success. The phrase, in print, at least, seems to have originated with the Irish writer Thomas Moore, whose 1835 edition of *The Works of Lord Byron* included the line: 'Saint Augustine . . . avoided the school as the plague.' Today, however, the expression has become so tired and overworked that it is best – well – avoided.

BABY-BOOMER GENERATION

A baby boom, a US term coined in the early 1940s, is any marked upsurge in the birth rate. 'Baby-boomers' (also originally American) refers specifically to the children born in the post-Second World War baby boom – that is, at, or within about seven years of, the end of the war. By the time the phrase gained currency in the 1970s there were baby boomers everywhere, and there still are. Thus *Time* magazine in January 1974: '"We" – the baby boomers – had the schools, the attention of the media [etc.].' Usually middle class, usually educated, and fuelled by a considerable, though not always justified, sense of entitlement, they travelled the world on credit cards, took advantage of vastly improving health services (for they knew how to deal with officialdom), turned the 1960s into a squat and shored-up hippiedom, listened to loud music and flocked to festivals in their thousands, demonstrated, did drugs, had sex, approved the Pill and deplored the Bomb, became yuppies, took most of the university places and all the decent jobs and pensions, and had retired or were retiring just as the present economic collapse took hold. Today they get free rides on buses, but the recession has hammered their pensions and investments, so the twilight years of many will be spent dependent upon their children, whose educational, career and financial prospects they have helped to destroy. Which is perhaps another good reason for retiring the phrase – for good.

Back to the drawing board

Meaning? That it's time to reassess; time to accept that the project has failed, or the client doesn't like the design and you have to try again. Generally, the phrase is uttered in tones of jocular resignation, and it does not always involve drawing boards, those tables used by draughtsmen, architects, and the like that are now being superseded by computer programs. The phrase is thought to have originated in a cartoon in *The New Yorker* of 1 March 1941 (some nine months before the US entered the Second World War), depicting a crashed aircraft towards which emergency services and military personnel are hurrying, with a single figure walking away, a roll of blueprints under his arm, saying to himself, 'Well, back to the old drawing board' (which earns him a dirty look from a senior officer). Overuse of the phrase has turned it into a tired cliché, especially as fewer and fewer people even know what a drawing board looks like, as computers move in. Bizarrely, though, the technology that consigned boards to the scrap heap ends up in the twenty-first century launched by the late Steve Jobs in March 2011, with the announcement, 'the iPad2 . . . will likely cause [Apple's rivals] to go back to the drawing board yet again.'

BAD-HAIR DAY

A day which starts badly when you wake up to discover your hair is in a bit of a mess and you can't do anything with it . . . and things only get worse from there. The phrase appeared first in print in 1998 in the *Press Democrat*, a daily paper published in California (where else?), but belongs really to the 1990s, gaining widespread popularity after featuring in an episode of the TV series *Buffy the Vampire Slayer*. Remember, this was the decade when we spent at least several million man-hours discussing the cultural importance of that layered-bob thing worn by Rachel in *Friends*, and when we were encouraged to spend huge amounts on our hairstyles with the reassurance '**Because I'm worth it**'. It was a post-Cold War, pre-War on Terror decade, when having bad hair was pretty much the worst it could get. In more recent times, the term was used in slightly dubious taste by headline writers covering the murder conviction in 2009 of Phil Spector, music genius but possessor of an indisputably bad mane. The phrase still has its uses to describe, as the *OED* puts it, 'a day on which everything seems to go wrong; a period (not necessarily a day) in which one feels unusually agitated, dissatisfied, or self-conscious, esp. about one's appearance or performance.' It is seriously misemployed, however, in descriptions of, say, being bombed in a **collateral damage** incident.

Ballpark figure

This is, we might say, an idiom as **American as apple pie**. Or at least its origins are. But its use has spread far and wide across the globe, the phrase spouted by sharply dressed executives (but with their ties loosened to suggest the red heat of business transactions) snapping, more often than not into their handsets, 'Hell! Give me a ballpark figure at least . . .' The first appearance in print of 'ballpark' to mean 'A broad area of approximation . . . a range within which comparison is possible, and in astronautics, the area within which a spacecraft is expected to return to earth', according to the *OED*, was on 21 August 1960, when the *San Francisco Examiner* reported that 'The *Discoverer XIV* capsule . . . came down 200 miles from the center of its predicted impact area, but still within the designated "ballpark" area.' That makes sense – a ballpark, or baseball stadium, is a large area and comfortingly familiar to US citizens as an analogy. Two hundred miles is infinitesimal when landing a spacecraft on earth, but when it comes to estimating, say, a profits shortfall? The required minimum of 122 metres (400 feet) from home plate to the centre in a baseball field (baseball stadiums vary in size) indicates that a ballpark is pretty large – and a ballpark figure therefore a *very* rough estimate. From 1967, the term appeared regularly in *The Wall Street Journal*; by the end of the twentieth century it had migrated across the Atlantic and beyond to be bandied about by those who have no idea how large – or even what – a ballpark is.

BATTLE OF THE BULGE

The Battle of the Bulge, also known as the Ardennes Offensive or, to the Germans, the Von Rundstedt Offensive, was one of the grimmest battles of the Second World War. Prompted by a desperate but initially successful German offensive undertaken in Belgium, France and Luxembourg between December 1944 and January 1945, it proved the bloodiest single battle of the war for US forces. By its end, both the Allied and German sides could count 100,000 dead, wounded or captured. Bearing all of that in mind, how has the term come to be the default tagline for any story featuring anyone (though usually a celebrity) trying to lose a bit of weight? Will Britney shed that spare 3 pounds before her tour starts? Will you get your bikini body in time for your holiday? Is Kim Kardashian carrying extra junk in that trunk? Frankly, who cares? This, we can be fairly sure, is not what the war was fought for, and the survivors from, say, the American forces who gallantly and successfully defended Bastogne have every reason to take offence.

Because I'm worth it

You have to hand it to L'Oréal, the world's largest cosmetics conglomerate, for it has stuck loyally with its slogan – originally used in advertisements for Preference hair colour – since 1971. At the time it was provocative (if a touch self-regarding), not least because the idea, then, of independent-minded women of high self-esteem was still a revolutionary one. Even so, the company has adapted it over the years. The campaign began as a first person 'I'm worth it' – which risked making customers fear that, while, say, Claudia Schiffer might be worthy, the rest of womankind could go hang. So in the mid-2000s in came 'you're', perhaps prompting thoughts of a bossy conglomerate dictating its terms via Scarlett Johansson. In 2009 'Because we're worth it' arrived apparently 'to create stronger consumer involvement in L'Oréal philosophy and lifestyle and provide more consumer satisfaction with L'Oréal products'. These days, 'I'm', 'You're' and 'We're' abound and, even worse, the phrase has been adapted, usually by journalists, to describe what is often called the 'Me Generation', as in this headline in *The Guardian* in February 2012: 'Bankers' bonuses – blame the "because I'm worth it" generation'. When a successful advertising catchphrase starts being used disapprovingly, it is almost certainly time to abandon it.

BENCHMARK

The original benchmark was a 'surveyor's mark cut in some durable material, as a rock, wall, gate-pillar, face of a building', the *OED* tells us. You may have seen such marks, typically a horizontal levelling line with a three-line arrow pointing, usually upwards, towards it – the whole looking a bit like a child's drawing of a three-legged stool. Nowadays 'benchmark' is possibly more often used in its figurative sense of 'a point of reference, a criterion', against which to compare or assess. *The Economist* of 18 May 1963 wrote, 'Foreign firms have failed to get . . . orders unless they have offered a price advantage of at least 50 per cent. This is the "benchmark".' While it is important to keep businesses up to the (bench-) mark, the term has become a cliché, used all too often without reference to any particular criterion, or mistakenly used to mean a target or aim – no way to promote excellence, yet as such even adopted into company names, whether they sell kitchens or insurance, to suggest superiority.

Best/Greatest thing since sliced bread

This cliché goes back at least to the 1950s, and is usually applied to some invention that is likely to improve people's lives – however one may feel about ready-sliced bread, which is, let's face it, not a patch on the real thing. Sliced bread was introduced to American consumers in 1933 by Wonder Bread, the inventor Otto Rohwedder having by then refined his bread-slicing machine so that it would also wrap the loaf to keep it fresh. It was promoted as 'the greatest step forward in the baking industry since bread was wrapped'. For many people it really was that, saving a great deal of time and effort. The origin of the phrase 'the best/greatest thing since sliced bread' is uncertain, but is likely to be based on the Wonder Bread promotion ('the greatest step . . . since bread was wrapped') and might have been coined by the comedian Red Skelton, who was quoted in the *Salisbury Times* (Maryland), 5 January 1952, as saying 'Don't worry about television. It's the greatest thing since sliced bread.' So well known as a cliché, this phrase is almost invariably uttered tongue-in-cheek – even when the speaker is promoting or praising the object or person in question. A heading in the *Australian Forest Industries Journal* (Plywood & Veneer) of October 1981 reads: 'Sheathing – the greatest thing since sliced bread!'

BETTER LATE THAN NEVER

The phrase dates in English from the early fourteenth century, but its origins are much earlier. In the first century BC, the Greek historian, writer and rhetorician Dionysius of Halicarnassus wrote, 'It is better to start doing what one has too late than not at all.' To anyone who has revised at the last minute for an exam, sent a reply to a wedding invitation far later than requested, or scraped into an important meeting after oversleeping, these are comforting words. However, there is surely not a more infuriating cliché on the end of which to find oneself. No one wants to wait an hour for a train only for a station announcer to proclaim boldly: 'Better late than never!' So why is it that so many people feel they can brush their own laziness, incompetence or sheer pig-headedness under the carpet by uttering these words to often incredulous ears? In 2010 the US government received twenty-seven offers of international help to clear up the BP *Deepwater Horizon* oil spill in the Gulf of Mexico before finally taking anyone up. 'Better late than never,' declared several supportive journalists. To which the anti-clichéist – indeed, any **right-thinking person** – can only reply 'Fiddlesticks!'(or perhaps something ruder, of which 'Cr★p!' would probably be the mildest). Because it would have been much better if such help had been accepted much earlier.

BETWEEN A ROCK AND A HARD PLACE

A vivid American phrase that overuse has worn down to a cliché. Similar to 'Between Scylla and Charybdis' (the sea monster and whirlpool of Greek mythology) and 'Between the Devil and the deep (blue) sea', the phrase describes a person's predicament when facing two options, equally grim and dangerous. The phrase was first recorded in the American Dialect Society's journal, *Dialect Notes*, V, 1921: 'To be between a rock and a hard place . . . to be bankrupt. Common in Arizona in recent panics; sporadic in California.' The 'recent panics' referred to the 'US Bankers' Panic' of 1907, which hit industry very badly. Following the First World War, however, the Arizona copper mines were enjoying enormous profits, not reflected in the miners' pay. Working conditions were terrible, and petitions from miners at the biggest copper mine at Bisbee for safer and better terms of employment were unsuccessful. In 1917 the miners went on strike. In the early hours of 12 July, almost 1,200 men were rounded up and forcibly deported to New Mexico, where they were abandoned. Between the hardships of the rock face and the homeless, jobless penury of a hard place, could the plight of these miners have given rise to the phrase? If today you lament that you are between a rock and a hard place, few will believe you are bankrupt and have nowhere to turn to, assuming rather that you are simply facing a tricky choice. The phrase has been done to death.

BIG PICTURE

Originally, the 'big picture' was the main feature at the cinema in the days of the B–movie. Nowadays it is the main feature of a given situation. The person who sees the 'big picture' is the one who *can* see the wood in the phrase 'You cannot see the wood for the trees,' the one able to take an overview and see everything and therefore make a better judgement. (That is, assuming that the details – the trees – are not important.) As early as 1942, US Lieutenant–Colonel Robert Allen Griffin defined his understanding of 'strategy': 'The term applies to the big picture; it is used in direction of campaigns . . . to win wars.' The big picture is quite often the **bottom line**. And the one who can see the big picture is a visionary and winner of wars. So naturally the phrase has become another hackneyed bit of business-speak, even used attributively as in 'So-and-so is a real big-picture boss.' But maybe those trees that make up the wood – the details that add up to arrive at the **bottom line** – should not be entirely forgotten: one diseased tree could bring down the whole wood.

BLACK-BOX/CREATIVE ACCOUNTING

BLACK-BOX/CREATIVE ACCOUNTING

Put very simply, in science a 'black box' is something that can be viewed solely in terms of its input, its output and the relationship between input and output – without what is going on inside it being visible to anyone. The term was first used around 1945, but only became more widely known when it was taken into computer technology. It was subsequently adopted into accounting terminology to describe a form of 'creative accounting', bursting into or maybe on to public consciousness in 2001 with the Enron scandal in the USA. In black-box accounting, highly and deliberately complex

33

accounting methods, with unnecessarily technical and tortuous language, are employed to hide unfavourable details and deflect close examination. Thus, the energy company Enron was believed to have made enormous profits, whereas in fact it had made huge losses. As the *Wall Street Journal*'s 'Heard on the Street' column of 23 January 2002 explained: black-box accounting is 'financial statements, like Enron's, that are so obscure that their darkness survives even the light of day'. While it cannot be termed ethical, black-box accounting is not illegal – as long as its creativeness follows the guidelines of the International Accounting Standards or Generally Accepted Accounting Principles. In Enron's case it didn't.

Blamestorming

First recorded in print in 1997, this witty adaptation of **brainstorming** refers to the propensity in some people, or some companies, as *Wired* magazine put it, 'to sit around and discuss why a deadline was missed or a project failed and who's responsible,' rather than actually try to sort out the problem. It's not an especially useful habit – witch-hunting is never attractive – but it's not an especially useful buzzword either, since it is now more often used to mean 'to apportion blame', rather than the full process of discussing that apportionment, arguably as a displacement activity (and, very often, in an attempt to deflect any blame from oneself). Like **It's not rocket science**, its usefulness and relevance have not outlived its undeniable cleverness.

BLOOD AND TREASURE

An expression that dates from the seventeenth century, but with earlier origins, and which became, as one commentator put it, 'the Iraq War's go-to cliché'. It is sometimes seen as 'lives and treasure', and refers to the cost, financial and human, of, usually, war, though it has also been used of the US space programme. The phrase was certainly known to Oliver Cromwell, and was used by Sir Henry Vane to denounce the latter's son, Richard: 'We have driven away the hereditary tyranny of the house of Stuart, at the expense of much blood and treasure . . .' In the eighteenth and nineteenth centuries it was used by, among others, John Adams and Thomas Jefferson, and the fifth president of the USA, James Monroe, deployed it in support of his famous Doctrine in 1823. Today, it has become tired from use in articles and programmes about the wars in Iraq and Afghanistan, and in the hand-wringing of politicians over the costs of those wars. Poetic and verging on the archaic – 'treasure' here does not mean treasure as most people understand the term, but a nation's exchequer – the expression has become wearisome almost to the point of meaninglessness.

BLUE-SKY THINKING

Blue skies, not a cloud to be seen. Allow your thoughts to soar unfettered into a clear untroubled sky, to range far and wide without preconceptions, to be creative, to dream up ideas . . . The origins of this piece of office jargon, most commonly heard in the UK, are obscure, but an early reference to it appeared in an Iowa newspaper, the *Oelwein Daily Register*, in April 1945: 'Real thinking. Speculation. Pushing out in the blue. Finding out [the facts] was what put me on to the theory of blue-sky thinking.' The idea behind blue-sky thinking is related to Edward de Bono's concept of lateral thinking in that individuals are encouraged to **think outside the box**, that is, unconventionally, from a different perspective. While it might have grown out of the adjective 'blue-sky', recorded in 1906 in the USA with the definition 'fanciful, impractical, having little or no value', in the UK this meaning has been abandoned in favour of the attractions of a clear blue sky. The US is more cautious, as may be seen from the definition in *Webster's*: '1. having little or no value (*blue-sky* stock); 2. not grounded in the realities of the present, visionary (*blue-sky* thinking).' According to a UK survey by YouGov, 49 per cent of those questioned believed that the use of terms such as this, **brainstorming** or **think outside the box** is on the increase as employees seek to impress their bosses. That's not blue-sky thinking.

BOOTS ON THE GROUND

This term – which literally refers to the presence of troops in an actual or potential theatre of combat – probably dates from the 1950s, and was certainly used by a British officer and counter-insurgency expert during the Malayan Emergency, 1948–60. It is in contrast to other forms of military action, such as area bombing or, nowadays, the deployment of pilotless drones. In the hands of politicians and journalists, however, the phrase has become less specific in meaning, often just referring to troop numbers, rather than combat troops in a zone of conflict. From there, and even less specifically, its use has spread until it sometimes means little more than people present: 'I was pleased to see so many boots on the ground at the annual school reunion' is hardly an appropriate usage, for here the meaning has been converted to something like the British phrase 'bums on seats' (US: 'fannies in the seats'). 'Combat' means soldiers as targets for other people, who can be shot at, or blown up. 'Boots on the ground' sounds marginally less intimidating than 'combat' but still conveys a rolled-up-shirtsleeves approach. The rise in popularity of the phrase possibly underlines the decline in popularity among the citizenry of actual military engagement.

BOTTOM LINE

'Bottom line is, you the finest,' goes the rapper Big Sean's 2011 song 'Marvin and Chardonnay'. 'What is he on about?' you might ask. Just as perplexingly, the *New Musical Express* remarked in 1992 that 'The bottom line is that we all love music and want to play it.' The phrase is a reference to the last (bottom) line of a company's financial statement, which shows its net profit or loss – undeniably an important detail. This definition has been extended to mean the final result or upshot, and subsequently it has come to mean the essential or most salient point of whatever is under consideration. As in this quotation from the *San Francisco Examiner* as early as 1967: 'George Murphy and Ronald Reagan certainly qualified because they have gotten elected. I think that's the bottom line.' For self-important executives the phrase is used to mean simply what they want to know: 'I don't want to hear what you have to say, I want to know the bottom line,' they might snap. That, after all, is what matters to them **at the end of the day** . . . A 1987 episode of the successful American television series *Murder, She Wrote* has the title *The Bottom Line Is Murder*. It has a point.

BRAIN DUMP

This phrase has its origins in 1950s computing, with 'to dump' meaning to copy data from one location to another – just as we nowadays back up our files and documents from an internal to an external hard drive, as a January 1956 issue of *Computers & Automation* explains: 'Dump, to transfer all or part of the contents of one section of computer memory into another section.' 'Brain dump', with its slightly alarming visual image, thus has the general meaning of transferring information, usually from an individual's mind (brain) to another individual, or recording it for one's own or another's use or edification, whether by means of the latest technology or by writing it down. A **brainstorming** session might include a brain dump – when all present put their ideas into a melting pot. Or a brain dump could be a 'Things To Do' list by another – puffed–up – name.

Brainstorming

This means little more than 'sitting around discussing', but in the jargon-loving world of business management it is far preferable, being more dramatic and hard–hitting. Better still, a brainstorming session might incorporate **blue–sky thinking**. The concept was devised in 1939 by an American advertising executive, Alex Faickney Osborn, who, finding his employees could come up with more and better ideas when they worked together, began running group thinking sessions. It caught on rapidly and the term became immensely popular. 'When our missing robot failed of location anywhere . . .' Isaac Asimov wrote in his 1947 short story 'Little Lost Robot', 'we brainstormed ourselves into counting the robots left . . .' In 1953, Osborn published a book, *Applied Imagination*, in which he described the methods and rules of brainstorming, and although subsequent research has failed to support his claim that brainstorming could double a group of individuals' creative output, many businesses remain firmly in favour of it. A word of caution: in the US, a brainstorm is 'a sudden clever idea' or what in the UK is known as a 'brainwave', whereas in the UK, 'brainstorm' can mean 'a moment or period in which one is suddenly unable to think clearly'. Whether this matters in a brainstorming session is a moot point . . . And *The Observer* newspaper of 26 June 2005 reported: '"Brainstorming", the buzzword used by executives to generate ideas among their staff, has been deemed politically incorrect by civil servants because it is thought to be offensive to people with brain disorders.' Which leads us to **political correctness (gone mad)**, and to the term's replacement in some workplaces with the even sillier 'thought shower'. (*See also* **Blamestorming**.)

BUCK STOPS HERE, THE

We owe this cliché originally to the saloons and riverboats of nineteenth-century America, although it was popularized by a no-nonsense US president in the early 1950s. In a poker game, when it was your turn to deal the cards, you had a buck placed in front of you. This was not, as you might be forgiven for thinking, a US dollar, but could be any small object used as a marker or counter, such as a pencil stub or a pocket knife. So when it was your turn to deal, the buck stopped with you. When you no longer had that responsibility, or if you opted out of dealing, you passed the buck to the next person. Thus Mark Twain in his semi-autobiographical *Roughing It* (1872): 'I reckon I can't call that hand. Ante and pass the buck.' Harry S. Truman, president of the USA from 1945 to 1953, kept a sign on his desk in the Oval

Office proclaiming that 'The BUCK STOPS here!', said to have been given to him by a prison warden and keen poker player (and which is several levels above 'You don't have to be mad to work here, but it helps'). Truman became president in the closing months of the Second World War, went on to oversee his country's involvement in the Korean War and its ascension to superpower status, and introduced the Fair Deal. He could well argue that he did indeed take ultimate responsibility for things. The problem today is that so many of those people most eager to throw this expression about are the sort of mealy-mouthed 'leaders of men' who speak the words at the same time as they are desperately striving to pass the buck on to some other sucker, if they can find one.

CATALYST FOR POSITIVE CHANGE

Consider catalyst: 'the action or effect of a substance in increasing the rate of a reaction without itself being consumed,' as the *OED* puts it. Then consider one of Australia's largest and finest universities. And then ponder why such a distinguished seat of learning has to advertise a post by stipulating that the successful applicant should be a 'catalyst for positive change'. What else could an applicant be? A catalyst for negative change who, once chosen, sets fire to the library, derides all that the university stands for, and embraces nihilism? That university, advertising in the *Times Higher Education Supplement*, is not alone; university advertisements seem to reflect a raging demand for such catalysts. Nor is the use of this pompous and largely meaningless cliché confined to the academic world. Other such catalysts to have been hailed in the press have included the Olympic Games, Hurricane Katrina, extra-marital affairs – and military action in Afghanistan.

CATCH-22

In 1961 Joseph Heller's *Catch-22,* about a group of American military flyers based in Italy in 1943, was published and went on to become one of the bestselling novels about the Second World War. Not everybody was enthusiastic – indeed the *Times Literary Supplement* suggested that what Heller had to say was 'spread very thinly on the ground'. But, in the anti-authoritarian 1960s – and ever since – a grubby copy of the novel under an arm said something anti-authoritarian about the arm's owner (a habit that quickly became wearisome in its own right). 'Catch-22' was an official condition that 'specified that a concern for one's safety in the face of dangers that were real and immediate was the process of a rational mind'. In Heller's novel Orr, a bomber pilot, 'would be crazy to fly more missions and sane if he didn't, but if he were sane he had to fly them. If he flew them he was crazy and didn't have to; but if he didn't want to he was sane and had to.' The modern world is beset with such pesky catches. However, the phrase is now often used – usually in the ugly form 'a Catch-22 situation' – to imply some minor dilemma ('Should I go to my cousin's wedding – meaning lying to take a day off work – or not go, and risk my rich uncle's wrath?'), rather than the efforts of an all-powerful authority to give its charges no option but to comply with a regulation. (*See also* **American as apple pie**. Interestingly, the first chapter of Heller's novel was published in 1955 in a literary magazine under the title *Catch-18*, and at various times *Catch-11*, *Catch-14* and *Catch-17* were mooted, before being discarded in favour of the now ubiquitous phrase.)

COLLATERAL DAMAGE

Collateral damage is about side-effects and the unintended consequences of actions. Reduced to its barest minimum, it means 'non-combatants killed or wounded in error by the military' or, if no one got hurt, 'hitting the wrong target'. It is, in short, a euphemism, used to disguise or diminish the very real consequences that result from the wrong target being hit by accident, and for that reason is a favourite phrase of military spokespeople. The term was in use in the early nineteenth century, but in the last two decades it has moved out of the military sphere, so that these days it can take in anything from the Eurozone crisis and company mergers to denial of service to legitimate users by website administrators. And then there is collateral damage and military commentators. Since Vietnam in the 1960s and subsequent wars in the Balkans, the Caucasus, the Middle East and Afghanistan, not to mention 'targeted strikes' and pilotless drones, violent death has another name. In military terms, collateral damage means people far away, often, though not always, with brown or black faces, dying because they happened to be in the wrong place. (*See also* **Stuff happens**.)

CONSIDER ONE'S POSITION, TO

Someone who is considering his position is in fact wondering whether or not to resign from his post, usually with the implication that if he does not do so he will be sacked. The use of the verb 'consider' in this meaning dates back to Chaucer in the fourteenth century, but its use as a euphemism for 'reflecting upon whether to jump before being pushed' dates from the second half of the twentieth century, and probably originated with press releases or other official or semi-official notices issued in an attempt to minimize the fall-out from some scandal. When deployed by the media it can seem to be almost a threat, as in this recent BBC News report on the phone-hacking scandal involving Rupert Murdoch's News Corporation, which quotes a senior Liberal Democrat politician who, referring to the then head of the Metropolitan Police's inquiry, stated: 'A failure of judgement on this [phone-hacking] case is, from professional grounds alone . . . a considerable reason for him to be considering his position.' (The officer in question did indeed resign.) Like most well-worn euphemisms, no one is fooled by it, so that if someone in authority says to you 'I think you should consider your position,' you know it's probably time to clear your desk, and perhaps think about whether you should **Spend more time with your family**.

CORPORATE DNA

Deoxyribonucleic acid – DNA – to put it simply, contains all the genetic codes that make up nearly all living organisms. As business-speak loves science, or at least science's terminology, which it borrows indiscriminately, a business – or corporation – is made up of corporate DNA. The term is thought to have been coined by the business-communications expert Ken Baskin in his 1998 book *Corporate DNA: Learning*

From Life, in which he looks at companies as if they were living organisms. That does not seem unreasonable, given that those who work for and are part of companies are living organisms, and the business world embraced the phrase joyously to mean a company's basic and unchanging composition, made up of 'core values', purpose, culture, personality, and so on, all of which supposedly get passed on to every new employee. It is, of course, highly unscientific nonsense. Every employee taken on by a corporation, however lowly, will slightly alter the 'unchanging DNA', and a new boss might alter it radically. Moreover, while change is not always necessary, the so-called DNA has to be changeable – what about the market's requirements? Or the current financial climate? Or environmental considerations? Don't want to be left behind or to lose customers, after all.

CRITICAL MASS

Another scientific term, it is difficult to understand how it escaped from nuclear physics into the world of business and seriously trite corporate-speak. It means 'the minimum mass of fissionable material that can sustain a nuclear chain reaction', and once that has been achieved, the end results can be anything from useful – as in a nuclear reactor generating electricity – to catastrophic: a nuclear explosion. By the late 1970s it had crossed over into business parlance, and it is also a favourite with the computer-software industry. In this looser usage it generally means the minimum amount of investment, or number of people needed to get an idea, a business or some other project off the ground, but from there the meaning has loosened further, until it is sometimes used just to mean a large number or large amount, without any sense of momentum. It is probably forgivable for a sports journalist to write of a play in American football that it had 'reached critical mass', resulting in the chain reaction of passes that leads to a goal. Similarly, an advertising campaign might be said to have reached critical mass once a slogan enters general usage (as, for instance, **'Because I'm worth it'**), for it has achieved a momentum beyond the original advertising brief. Politicians, too, sometimes talk of some popular movement 'achieving critical mass', meaning that it has gained, and continues to gain, support to the extent that it can no longer be ignored. Even so, this presupposes that readers confronted with the phrase have some basic understanding of nuclear physics; many, if not the majority, don't – as good a reason as any for dropping it.

Cut to the chase

This expression originates in the US film industry, its earliest appearance in print being a script direction for the 1930 film *Show Girl in Hollywood*, based on the novel *Hollywood Girl* by the satirist J. P. McElvoy: 'Jannings escapes . . . Cut to chase.' In 1944 the *Winnipeg Free Press* reported that the scriptwriter Helen Deutsch had a note stuck on her wall that read: 'When in doubt, cut to the chase.' Advice that still stands today, with a chase of some sort central to the plot of so many action films. Figurative use followed not that long after: the Massachusetts newspaper *The Berkshire Evening Eagle* announced bluntly in February 1947: 'Let's cut to the chase. There will be no tax relief this year.' The glamour of its derivation, for those who know it, and for those who don't, the arcaneness of the phrase soon turned it into an expression the busy executive – or would-be busy executive – likes to use to indicate that he is very busy and has no time for idle chit-chat or details – what he wants is to get down to business, to get to the point, the **bottom line**. As *Marketing* magazine of 16 December 1999 put it: 'Stop bullsh*tting and cut to the chase.'

CUTTING EDGE

Until the nineteenth century the cutting edge meant only that – the sharp edge of a blade. From there it came to mean 'a dynamic, invigorating, or incisive factor or quality', the hard edge – as in H. G. Wells's *Mr Britling* (1916): 'a prosperous comfortable man who had never come to the cutting edge of life' – and thence to 'the latest or most advanced stage in the development of something'. It can be applied to nearly everything, as in the body: 'The hand is the cutting edge of the mind' (Jacob Bronowski, *The Ascent of Man*, 1973); attitude: 'As individualism . . . diminishes in favor of a more cooperative type of community life, the intense drive to win . . . will doubtless lose its cutting edge' (E. D. Mitchell and B. S. Mason, *Theory of Play*, 1934); film: 'The Independent Spirit Awards . . . are often given for cutting-edge films which are not necessarily box-office draws' (*Courier-Mail*, Brisbane, Australia, 25 March 1996); music, education, fashion, cookery (*Food & Beverage* magazine keeps you 'on the Culinary Cutting Edge') . . . And of course technology, which must always be at the cutting edge. 'In this post we present stunning examples of cutting-edge technology which is already reality today or will become reality in 2008,' announced smashingmagazine.com on 4 February 2008. How cutting-edge is that technology today? Devalued by overuse to mean 'the most up to date', the phrase itself has lost its sharpness. Indeed, when referring to the very, *very* latest technology, the expression is now 'bleeding-edge'.

DEAD-CAT BOUNCE

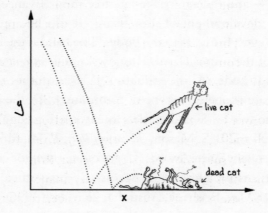

As in 'Even a dead cat will bounce if dropped from high enough,' the phrase refers to a temporary recovery in the value of a share or shares, or an entire stock market, after a substantial fall. It dates from 1985, and was first used of the financial markets of Malaysia and Singapore, which experienced a short-lived rise in share prices after a considerable drop brought about by the recession of that year. Inevitably, such a graphic, bite-sized phrase was soon adopted by Wall Street and London's City, and picked up by journalists, so that it lost much of its specific meaning; an article in the *Sydney Morning Herald* in April 2011, about the Swedish car manufacturer Saab, said the company had 'survived a near-death experience . . . although the jury is still out on whether it's a dead-cat bounce'. From there it spawned other bounces, as noted by the online Phrase Finder: 'The phrase seems to have struck a chord and other "bounce" phrases have emerged, notably "Baghdad bounce". This is the rise in popularity that both George Bush and Tony Blair enjoyed following the fall of Baghdad' in April 2003. (It was a 'bounce' because their popularity fell back once it was realized that the withdrawal of Allied forces from Iraq was likely to be long delayed.) The point about a dead-cat bounce is that it is insignificant, so to use it of a more substantial recovery – in anything – weakens it further. It is probably best left to its financial usage, not least because a sentence like 'His cancer treatment has enjoyed a bit of a dead-cat bounce' is arguably as tasteless as it is infelicitous.

Deep dive

Are we talking *The Hunt for Red October* here? *Ice Station Zebra*? *On the Beach*? Sonar pings? Air bubbling noisily to the surface? Decisions in the face of death? No, we are talking people in offices planning to explore or investigate matters which, important as they may be, do not involve life-or-death dramas. 'We did a deep dive on those figures yesterday – it's time to **push the envelope**.' In 2007 a US and international design and innovations consultancy, the IDEO Group, developed a **brainstorming** technique called DeepDive, its purpose being 'to rapidly immerse a group or team into a situation for problem solving or idea creation'. And when the American business magazine *Fortune* was revamped in 2010, it would focus more, its managing editor said, on 'long-form, deep-dive journalism'. In general, non-specific usage this is one of those expressions that sound good but mean little. Submarines and scuba-diving sound more fun.

DIRTY TRICKS

What began in the 1950s as CIA slang for the agency's covert operations (its plans division would, by the early 1960s, eventually come to be referred to wryly as the Department of Dirty Tricks) has become one of the most overworked phrases in the commercial, political and journalistic worlds. Of course, sometimes it can be the most apt of terms. President Richard Nixon's attempt to gain an advantage over his Democrat rivals by waving through a break-in at the Watergate complex in Washington DC is almost the very definition of a dirty trick. But in a post-modern twist, an unprovable accusation of dirty tricks can itself be a potent dirty trick to discredit an opponent. In recent times we have the example of Julian Assange, founder of the Wikileaks website. Having achieved global fame by publishing vast quantities of classified documents, he himself was hit by allegations of sexual assault in Sweden in 2010. This was, he argued, a dirty trick perpetrated by enemies with agendas. Amid the mélange of accusations and counter-accusations, the truth becomes very hard to identify. But that is the problem with tricks – they are all about deception. The term is really a journalistic cliché, and is often broadly applied to clandestine intelligence work in general, whether involving dirty-trickery or not.

Downshifting

'Downshift' began life in late-1940s America, and means a change from a higher to a lower gear in or on any vehicle equipped with gears (its UK equivalent is 'to change down'). By the early 1960s it had transferred into US business, meaning to slow down or slacken off, or to reduce something in size or scope, somewhat akin to **downsizing**. By the 1980s, however, although sounding like another word for downsizing, or office jargon for demotion, the meaning had shifted again, in reference to individuals who choose to lead simpler lives, thereby escaping the rat race of office and career, and reducing the 'stress, overtime, and psychological expense that may accompany [them]', in the words of the authors of a 2007 paper, 'Downshifting Consumer', in *The Annals of the American Academy of Political and Social Science*. It does not necessarily mean giving everything up and moving to the country to live an uncomplicated life – it may just involve changing to a less well-paid but less demanding job, and reducing the size of your house, the number of cars you own, the amount of money you spend, usually unnecessarily. It may mean **spending more time with your family**; or it can be because you have fewer family members dependent upon you (children leaving home, or a death), so you can afford to take time off. For some it works, for others not; for some it is not that voluntary but comes as a reaction to changes at the workplace, or because they can't stand their work, or they've been 'let go' . . . The term is vague – a cliché used to cover any apparent downward trend in lifestyle while conjuring up visions of a happy, less materialistic, less taxing life.

DOWNSIZING

One of the most weaselly of all weasel words, this euphemism burrowed out of computerworld and swam from the USA across the Atlantic in the mid-1980s. However, it seems first to have appeared in print in reference to the US auto industry in the mid-1970s, when it was employed to mean, literally, building smaller cars to make them lighter and more economical, to meet market and government demands. Today, there are no doubt bluff, honest technicians harmlessly upgrading or 'downsizing' their computers, and people 'downsizing' their homes (although why they can't just move to a smaller property remains unclear). But by the end of the 1970s the word had come to be used as a euphemism for reducing the size or importance of something, which almost invariably results in people losing their jobs. Today, nine times out of ten, the word means – well, your job has been de-emphasized, concluded, ended, got rid of, terminated – downsized.

DRAW A LINE UNDER

A school pupil might write down the answer to a maths problem, draw a line under it, and go on to the next. Or perhaps an accountant will check the figures on the **bottom line** and draw a line under them. The figurative meaning, in both the UK and the USA, is that the matter is finished and you will not have to think about it again. The matter in question, incidentally, is something that does not generally reflect well upon someone. A boss might say to an employee guilty of some misdemeanour: 'All right: we will draw a line under that' (with the subtext 'but do it again and you're out'). Or it may be an effort to put something behind you, generally a failure, a disaster or controversy, like the Iraq War. 'The combination of not giving the weapons inspectors more time, and then the weapons not being found . . . led to a catastrophic loss of trust for us, and we do need to draw a line under it,' Ed Miliband, now leader of the UK's Labour Party, told *The Guardian* in May 2010 (subtext: 'Please forget that Labour could ever have done something so rash and costly'). President Obama, too, might have had voters in mind, the journalist Spencer Ackerman implied in November 2011: 'If it's really the case that the US is truly drawing a line under the [Iraq] war, as Obama is promising and the White House is reaffirming, then McCain's not going to get any happier.' (Senator John McCain, a Republican, had been Obama's opponent in the 2008 presidential campaign.)

DRILL DOWN, DRILLDOWN

What is it about business clichés? It's not enough that their users ape senior military commanders or hard-bitten soldiers, lithe, tough sportsmen or brilliant scientists, they now want to appropriate the mantle of oilmen. We owe 'drill down' to IT, and it means to perform a detailed search of folders on a computer, in order to find a specific file or files. No doubt a long and tedious business requiring great skill and concentration, but hardly analogous with sinking a drill bit thousands of feet into the earth. The phrase, in this sense, originated in the early 1990s, but soon transferred into more general business usage, thereby blunting its meaning, and often with predictably risible results: 'Okay, I want a drilldown on his employment record' is only a self-important way of saying 'Run a check.' (For those really interested – or unable to sleep – Wikipedia has this: 'The field of managerial economics uses the term "Drill Down" to explain exciting but technical aspects of operations research and regression analysis.') To summarize: to perform a 'drilldown' (for some reason the noun usually appears as one word) is to carry out an exhaustive search of a computer. So when not fantasizing lives beneath the ocean wave (*see* **deep dive**), our heroes reappear as sturdy oilmen, burrowing into the shale and hardrock of – of – uh, folders on the desktop of a computer, going through databases, finding information. Hardly the wildcatters of the corporate world.

Elephant in the Room, The

A colourful expression used to mean any obvious problem or controversial issue that is ignored or avoided, usually because to discuss it would be uncomfortable. There are elephants standing in for alcoholic parents, and for kids not coming out as gay to their mothers, and for Western governments selling arms that are used to put down democratic protests. The elephants showed up in the USA in the 1950s as symbolic of the thing everyone knows and no one will talk about. They started gathering in greater numbers in the 1980s, formed into herds and have been stampeding around the language ever since. Thus *The New York Times* in August 2004: 'When it comes to the rising price of oil, the elephant in the room is the ever-weakening United States dollar.' Perhaps there are just more secrets or embarrassments to conceal. The phrase still has its uses, but is best avoided if all that is meant is something that is not much discussed.

EMOTIONAL ROLLER-COASTER

The phrase was once useful as a colourful analogy for the dips and peaks and sudden swoops in the feelings of someone undergoing some kind of emotional crisis – an intense love affair, say, or the experience of being suddenly dumped, or, more tragically, the death of someone close. Sadly, it is now completely debased, having long ago become the first cliché to be trotted out whenever such matters are discussed, often during TV or magazine interviews. It is a staple of celebs (not necessarily, or even usually, of the **A-list** variety) who, when asked, for instance, how they have coped after having been left (subtext: dumped) for someone else (subtext: someone younger/richer/better-looking/nicer), will generally reply 'Well, y'know, I feel as though I've been on an emotional roller-coaster.' He or she may then add 'But I'm coming out of it now,' depending on how much sympathy is being sought. (It is a slightly worrying thought that the great English humorist P. G. Wodehouse, the creator of Jeeves and Bertie Wooster, and so much else, may have started the rot in his 1962 novel *Service With a Smile*: 'Her emotions were somewhat similar to those of a nervous passenger on a roller coaster at an amusement park . . .') Time to alight from the roller-coaster, perhaps employing the much older English expression 'up and down' instead, which has a certain uncomplaining insouciance to it.

END JUSTIFIES THE MEANS, THE

This phrase, often incorrectly attributed to the Florentine political philosopher of the fifteenth and sixteenth centuries, Nicolò Machiavelli, was in fact coined – in Latin – in the seventeenth century by the German theologian Hermann Busenbaum. It is a favourite of hard-nosed businessmen and ambitious politicians – such people do not have time for sentiment. They are decisive. They want *results* – the **bottom line** – and as long as those results are satisfactory it doesn't matter how they are obtained. 'Just do it,' they might say. 'I don't care how you do it – just get it done!' No doubt the insider dealer, seeing the profits mounting for his clients, believes the end will justify the means. But the day it all goes wrong, all the money is lost, his clients are ruined and he finds himself in deep trouble, will he be so sure? True, morally questionable actions are sometimes necessary to reach a morally right outcome. But morality is not too often a concern. The often-heard phrase is generally uttered mindlessly – a kind of verbal shrug to deter uncomfortable questions. It might be well to be wary of those who spout it.

ENVELOPE, ON THE BACK OF AN

An overworked phrase that seems to denote a striking casualness and propensity to be laid-back: 'I'll just jot down some notes on the back of this envelope . . .' Yes, sometimes things really can be that simple. The design for the Sydney Opera House allegedly started out on the back of that envelope, while the Italian physicist Enrico Fermi made some of his calculations that way to emphasize 'that complex scientific equations could be approximated within an order of magnitude using simple calculations' – so-called 'Fermi

Questions' or 'back-of-the-envelope calculations' (he went on to win a Nobel Prize, just to hammer home his point). Others, though, perhaps lack Fermi's skill. 'You and I could write the solution to Social Security problems,' said Senator John McCain during his campaign for the White House in 2008, 'on the back of an envelope.' The US electorate were not so sure. And, while it is a romantic and appealing notion, Abraham Lincoln did not jot down what became the Gettysburg Address on the back of an envelope. Today the phrase is used to mean any rough-and-ready plan or computation, although properly it means something that is a good deal better than a guess, but not yet an accurate calculation or fully worked-up proposal or design.

FAILURE IS NOT AN OPTION – *SEE* NOT AN OPTION

FAT CAT

Consider the feline: glistening golden fur perhaps, a fine set of whiskers, a contented yawn, a rhythmic purr . . . Why should this admirable creature become the focus of others' anger? Originating in 1920s USA, the term was originally applied to political backers: 'These capitalists have what the organization needs – money to finance the campaign. Such men are known in political circles as "Fat Cats"' (F. R. Kent, *Political Behavior*, 1928). 'Fat' because they are wealthy and live the good life, and 'cat' simply for the rhyme. By the 1970s the use of the term was growing on both sides of the Atlantic – *Flying* magazine refers in 1971 to 'Those who view the business jet as a smoke-belching, profit-eating chariot of the fat cat.' Fat cats grew up everywhere throughout the next two decades – financiers, industrialists, businessmen, plump felines all – and now, with the worldwide recession, have been found to be responsible for every financial disaster going. They are the cats we love to hate. 'It was,' said the distinguished British composer Sir Peter Maxwell Davies in 2011, 'the fat cats and bankers who got us into this mess.' 'I did not run for office to be helping out a bunch of fat-cat bankers on Wall Street,' announced President Obama during a 2009 CBS *60 Minutes* interview. And the Scottish *Daily Record* headlined a February 2012 news item 'Lloyds [Bank] claw back £1.5m in bonuses from fat-cat bosses as punishment for mis-sold insurance.' 'Claw'?

FEELGOOD FACTOR

Anything that promotes itself as 'feelgood' must attract interest, especially among today's populations that are so very solicitous towards their own feelings. As defined by the *OED*, the feelgood factor is that which 'induces or seeks to induce (often unwarranted) feelings of well-being, confidence, or ease'. As such, most things could probably be found to include a feelgood factor – from bodily comforts to more spiritual ones – but, as embraced by politicians, it could be made pervasive: vote for me and every aspect of your life will feel good. As early as 15 May 1977, *The New York Times Magazine* was remarking dryly, 'The latest aberration in the American pursuit of happiness is the feelgood movement,' and a few days later a headline in *The Washington Post* read: 'Test of Carter's "Feel Good" Foreign Policy is Workability.' More recently, in the UK, *The Times* of 28 July 1999 reported, 'Consumers are fuelling a summer housing and credit boom as the "feel-good" factor returns.' That was a little over-optimistic. The phrase is now everywhere, although it might be worth remembering that it originated from the American term 'Dr Feelgood', defined in the *OED* as 'a physician who readily prescribes mood-enhancing drugs, such as amphetamines, especially for non-medicinal use; hence, any doctor who provides short-term palliatives rather than a more effective treatment or cure,' and enough of a problem for *Newsweek* to announce in December 1972 that 'The best way to guard against Feelgoods and charlatans is for the medical profession to keep its own house in order.'

FIREFIGHTING/PUTTING OUT FIRES

A dramatic expression – which has guaranteed its adoption by many management types in the UK especially, where it seems to have originated during the 1990s. In the US the phrase is usually 'putting out fires'. A fire is an emergency and has to be dealt with at once to avert calamity. Businesses have emergencies – not as life-threatening or dangerous to property, but similarly unforeseen and urgent. A security breach, a lost file, hardware failure, broken coffee machine, colleague taken ill . . . dealing with them – usually when you have much else to attend to, such as your work – has come to be called 'firefighting', 'putting out fires' or, occasionally, 'fire drill'. On a larger scale, corporations and institutions have to put out fires that come in the form of, say, impending worldwide political or financial crises. The economics editor of *The Guardian* declared optimistically on 5 February 2012: 'Financial markets have had a rip-roaring start to 2012. Fire-fighting by the European Central Bank (ECB) has eased fears that the Eurozone will slide into a severe recession this year.' Management experts are not impressed, suggesting that all these figurative fires may reflect lack of organization and planning. Of course, there was a time when companies employed people whose job it was to deal with all those little emergencies – before businesses went in for **downsizing**.

-Gate

In 1972 a building complex named Watergate, situated in an area aptly named Foggy Bottom on the banks of the Potomac River in Washington, DC, was at the centre of the USA's biggest political scandal – and gave a new meaning to an innocuous English noun. As a snappy suffix, '-gate' soon came to be used instead of 'scandal'. The earliest recorded example dates from August 1972 in a report in *National Lampoon*, of a rumoured financial scandal in the Soviet Union: 'Implicated in "the Volgagate" are a group of liberal officials.' The following year a French journalist, speaking of a fraudulent scheme to sell cheap wine as expensive Bordeaux, said: 'You'll think it is exaggerating to say this, but the US had Watergate and now we have our winegate.' The floodgates – so to speak – were opened, and over the following decades there have been countless '-gates', often but by no means always involving politics, and mostly in the USA and the UK: Totegate, Tunagate, Irangate, Billygate, Squidgygate, Camillagate, Monicagate, Cablegate, Climategate are just a few. Hack- or Hackergate, the News International phone-hacking scandal which led to the closure of the British Sunday newspaper, the *News of the World*, in July 2011, has been raging since 2006. It might be worth noting that the use of '-gate' was promoted by President Nixon's former speechwriter and *New York*

Times columnist William Safire, who coined numerous '-gates' – it is thought as a way of minimizing the enormity of Watergate. 'My best,' he later said, 'was the encapsulation of a minor . . . scandal as doublebillingsgate.' So, really, a nonsensical term, whose nonsensical grammar is underlined, as the British comedians David Mitchell and Robert Webb pointed out in their sketch show *That Mitchell and Webb Look,* by the fact that nowadays Watergate would be called 'Watergategate', since plain 'Watergate' would refer to a scandal about water.

Get a life

Oh, get a life!

This little phrase – a kind of catch-all insult or disparaging put-down – goes back to the 1980s, its first appearance in print, according to the *OED*, in an article in *The Washington Post* dated 23 January 1983: '[the movie] *Valley Girl* was, like, ohmigod, it was last year, fer sure! I mean, get a life!' (*Valley Girl* was released in April 1983!) Occasionally used of oneself, in a tone of sad resignation – 'I never go out: I should get a life' – the phrase is more often a mindless insult flung at someone whose life and interests do not accord with those of the speaker. Occasionally the speaker may feel they are giving good advice in the sense of 'Stop worrying about unimportant details – get a life'. William Shatner, Captain Kirk of *Star Trek*, appearing on *Saturday Night Live* in December 1986, is shown in a skit addressing a group of Trekkies: 'Get a life, will you, people! I mean for crying out loud, it's just a TV show!' (It was a spoof – supposedly.) Acceptable perhaps where it is aimed at somebody who is interfering in the lives of others, the phrase is generally employed by those who lack imagination, vocabulary and good manners to imply a (non-existent) superiority over others and tell them they are boring and lead boring lives, and that they should have the same likes, dislikes, interests, lack of wit and bigotry as the speaker.

GET OVER IT!

As part of a sentence, 'get over' is an ordinary phrase, appearing in such statements as 'He's got flu, but I hope will get over it soon,' or as in the phrase's earliest known appearance in print, in Guy Miège's *Great French Dictionary*, 1687, 'They cannot get over the Prejudice of Education.' Some time in the 1990s, however, 'get over it' became a stand-alone phrase, its tone at best firm, more often than not exasperated, impatient, intolerant, harsh even; its meaning oscillating between 'accept it', 'get used to it' and 'overcome it'. An early example was in an article by the American writer Anna Quindlen syndicated in a number of US newspapers in November

1992: 'There will be people who complain that they didn't elect her [Hillary Clinton]. Get over it.' Gay communities took advantage of the phrase's pithiness in their 1990s slogan 'We're here, we're queer. Get over it', and the later 'Some people are gay. Get over it!' For the US soldier and statesman Colin Powell it is a maxim for anger management – 'Get mad, then get over it,' a rule he expounds in his 2012 book on leadership. Exhortatory doggerel – 'It's all part of life; it will help you grow stronger,/But this "pity party" of yours can't last any longer' – introduces 9 March as 'Get Over It Day'. But twenty years or so of overuse have made the phrase a cliché. Even so, its insensitivity cannot be overlooked. If you have to use it, be sure of what it is that you think the other person should get over.

GO FOR THE LOW-HANGING FRUIT

This expression conjures up images of orchards of trees with their branches weighed down by ripening fruit. At best, however, it is a cliché advocating common sense, at worst, it is cynical advice, the fruit in question being defined in the *Oxford Pocket Dictionary of Current English* as 'a thing or person that can be won, obtained, or persuaded with little effort'.

In print, the phrase goes as far back as 1984, appearing in an article in the American journal *Computer Decisions* extolling the usefulness of electronic storage in that it saves a great deal of time: '[He] expects corporate communications will be able to harvest even more benefits in the future. "So far," he says, "we're only grabbing the low-hanging fruit."' Since then it spread through the English-speaking world, especially in business and politics. In the UK, an article in *The Daily Telegraph* in November 2011 laments 'If the government can't grab the low-hanging fruit, we're never going to get growth,' referring to the government's decision not to reform the bill that prevents the redevelopment of existing property for different purposes. While in the USA, NASA has identified the 'low-hanging fruit' in climate change ('Rocket scientists say warming reduction isn't rocket science') – the simpler, more basic efforts that can be made to reduce damaging emissions. Picturesque as it might be, the expression is still a cliché – worse, it is not necessarily true. Critics suggest that there may be even greater rewards just a little higher up. Fruit-pickers point out that the best and ripest fruit is at the top and should be picked first – a little more time and effort results in something better. Besides which, someone who always goes for the low-hanging fruit – the easy option – might be assumed by others to be idle and unambitious.

Going forward

A somewhat pompous way of saying 'in the future', 'looking ahead', 'from now on' or 'to move on', this piece of businessman's cant is used, as often as not, to establish the speaker's credentials as someone thrusting, go-ahead, and *terribly* important. Its use is annoying because, of course, the speaker is not going forward; metaphorically or literally, he or she is trapped in an airless, low-ceilinged 'conference room' having a discussion with colleagues or clients. And what the phrase often actually indicates is the speaker's strong desire to stop discussing some problem or crisis – in other words, to change the subject. It is relatively recent in this usage, but its very looseness of meaning, coupled with the fact that, if removed from a sentence, there is usually no alteration in meaning or clarity at all, demonstrate its complete worthlessness, and it is much hated as a result. Let *BBC News Magazine* have the last word: 'It seems that the less one has to say, the more likely one is to reach for a *going forward* as a crutch. Politicians find it comforting for this reason. "We are going forward," poor Hillary Clinton said just before the last, fatal primary [in June 2008], when it became indisputable that she was going nowhere of the kind.' It is sometimes heard as 'moving forward', which is every bit as bad.

GREY AREA

Once there were meanings in the term. In the 1960s newspapers in New York and London criticized governmental policy towards 'grey areas', places which planners did not designate as slums, but which needed redevelopment. By the 1970s, countries like Yugoslavia and Austria, trapped between the Eastern Bloc and the NATO countries, had become grey areas. While, in South Africa, as the *Toronto Star* of 6 June 1999 reported, the unravelling of the Group Areas Act, which restricted people to neighbourhoods according to their colour, led to so-called grey areas, where anyone could live, regardless of colour. The phrase, which first appeared in print in the late 1940s means 'an ill-defined situation or field': neither black nor white, good nor bad, neither one thing nor another – and always slightly foggy. By the early 1950s the greyness began to spread everywhere, adopted eagerly by governments and official bodies, as the undefinable, the 'we have not made up our minds', the 'we are not sure', the 'not quite this, not quite that', seeping into everything from taxation and sexual discrimination to tennis players' appearance money and the US Star Wars missile programme. Will society ever see the back of the phrase? Hmm, well that too is a gre—

HANDS ARE TIED, MY (OR 'HIS', 'HER' ETC.)

I'd like to help, madam, but ...

No, they're not, as is patently obvious. The phrase has been used figuratively to mean that someone is not free to act as they would like for a very long time. Thomas Fuller, writing in 1642 about skirmishes between the French (led by 'this virago' Joan of Arc) and the English in the fifteenth century, remarks about the English being worsted: 'When God intends a Nation shall be beaten, he ties their hands behind them.' There could, of course, have been no other reason why the English lost . . . It was not until the late nineteenth century, however, that the phrase really caught on, and not until more recently that government and bureaucracy have seen its true potential as a face-saver. Today, this overused expression is no more than a slick excuse, especially when served up with a lavish helping of insincerity: 'I am so sorry,' says the bureaucrat or local politician who has deigned to talk to you, 'I truly believe in the **hands-on** approach and, trust me, **I know where you are coming from**; I'd really like to help you, but I'm afraid my hands are tied.' At which point, like any **right-thinking** person, you should walk out.

HANDS-ON

Not a reference to an overly tactile individual; a new employee need not back away when told that the boss takes a hands-on approach. Now more often used in the figurative sense of 'participating, involved', the phrase 'hands-on' was originally first applied, in the USA, simply to the use – having the hands on a keyboard – of an organization's computer in the days when computers were rare and enormous. The first appearance in print was in an article on the Massachusetts Institute of Technology in *The Times* of 27 October 1969: 'Elsewhere there are perhaps half a dozen IBM 1130s . . . used for "hands-on" calculations by students.' Since then the term has extended to cover just about anything in which you can participate – you might have hands-on experience of baking; of education (you stand in front of a class and teach, rather than write theoretical tomes); hands-on experience of running a company (you don't just sit aloofly in your grand office and demand the **big picture** and **ballpark figures**) – you might even be seen as somewhat interfering, but you get results, according to *Fortune* magazine, 31 December 1978: 'Through hands-on management and attention to the **bottom line**, the chief executive who got his job by accident has transformed the company.' The popularity of the phrase, with its **user-friendly**, homely overtones, has led to a revival of its earlier and literal meaning – thus there is hands-on learning in science, which means students conduct experiments themselves, or hands-on museums where people are allowed to touch or use the exhibits.

HANDS-OFF

And it would seem that anything that is not hands-on is hands-off. Foreign policy could be hands-off – *The Daily Chronicle* of 23 January 1902, for instance, did not agree with the stance of the British Prime Minister, David Lloyd George: 'A protest must be made against the hands-off policy,' while *The Economist* of 10 September 2011 noted, ' . . . the recent upheaval in the Arab world has put unusual stress on [China's] much-vaunted hands-off policy when it comes to others' affairs.' So could operating machinery: as early as 1932 *Flight* magazine remarked that 'By means of the adjustable tail plane the machine can be trimmed to fly "hands off".' And as for that interfering **hands-on** manager – since the 1990s there has been growing support for the hands-off manager – the one who lets employees act as they see fit. Hands – on, off or tied – should perhaps best be kept out of discussions.

HARDBALL, TO PLAY

Literally, to play baseball, as distinct from softball, which uses a larger ball, pitched underarm, and so is seen as a game for children and women. American – obviously – in origin, the word hardball, which dates from the late nineteenth century, fell increasingly out of use in the course of the twentieth, but survives in the figurative use of this expression, which originated in the early 1970s. In this sense, it refers to 'tough, uncompromising dealings or activity (esp. in political contexts)', so that by April 1985 *The New Yorker* was writing, in reference to the fact that Republican politicians who did not support President Reagan's programmes could not expect help with re-election, 'Such "hardball" is not new, but it is not Reagan's style.' Adopted into business language, the phrase, which carries overtones of unfairness as well as ruthlessness, is often favoured by the kind of senior executive who feels he needs to stress that he is playing the rough, tough man's game, rather than the safer, softer kid's version. It often carries an element of threat – 'Okay, if you want to play hardball . . .' – and can sound extraordinarily silly, as in this line from a *Fortune* magazine article in April 1983: 'If anyone wants to play hardball, [this company] can operate in the 5% to 6% range and still be profitable, because its costs are so lean.' Its usage has crossed over into British English, mainly in business and journalism, which is rather like hearing a US senator or the CEO of an American company use a cricketing metaphor.

HARD-WIRED

Yet another gift from computing, 'hard-wired' dates from the late 1960s, and refers to a permanent connection that cannot be changed by programming. There are other technical variations on this meaning, but within a very few years the term had transferred to other fields, notably in reference to the brain and its function, as in an article in *Scientific American* in June 1975, referring to the connection between eye and brain: 'The product of "hard-wired", or fixed, visual pathways originating at the retina and terminating in the cortex.' By extension, it came to mean 'genetically determined or compelled,' and this is where the trouble started, for it proved to be a short step from 'fight-or-flight responses are hard-wired in the human brain' to the American novelist Rick Moody writing that 'trying to make really good prose is hard-wired into my personality'. No it isn't – as admirable as his statement is, writing is learned, not innate, behaviour, and is no more hard-wired into us than are, say, the rules of baseball. The phrase is much used by journalists and businessmen, to the extent that it has been weakened to the point where it now means not much more than being single-minded about something, as in 'She's hard-wired to selling.'

HEADS-UP

'You are a military man, Langley, and no doubt like to see your regiment look well on parade, "Heads up" and all that.' When Anna Sewell's *Black Beauty* was published in 1877, the phrase was a military order – pay attention, be alert, look smart! In the US, it was used to mean 'Pay attention!' or 'Watch out!', then by extension as an adjective meaning 'Skilful, alert, in the know'; here is the *New Smyrna* (Florida) *News* in November 1913: 'He was always right on the job, and looking "heads up".' By the 1980s the phrase had started to take on the meaning of 'a warning' or 'a briefing': 'He gave the staff a heads-up that the boss was on her way'; 'I need a heads-up on the latest financial projections.' Cryptic, versatile and snappy, it has become one of the overused buzz-phrases of the business world, not helped by the woolly ambiguity of its meaning.

Hit the ground running

Used figuratively, this phrase has a history that goes back to the 1940s, but was honed and polished in that factory of tortured English, the Pentagon. It indicates youth, brimming over with vigour, paratroopers springing out of the sky, helicopters disgorging, soldiers lost in ditches, broken ankles . . . But in politics it means to be ready to work immediately on a new activity. Hence an ideal expression to be used by the new, and sixty-nine-year-old, US President, Ronald Reagan, when he took office in 1981.

'Houston, we have a problem'

Just how many memorable phrases can one jinxed space flight generate? On 13 April 1970, Captain Jim Lovell was leading the Apollo 13 space mission, following Apollo 11's Neil Armstrong and the July 1969 landing on the moon (*see* **'One small step for man'**). At eight minutes past nine in the evening, Houston time, crew member Jack Swigert said the words which, with a change of tense for the movie *Apollo 13* (1995; *see also* **Not an option**), went into history and some terrible headlines for ever more: 'Okay, Houston,' he announced, 'we've had a problem here,' and the phrase was repeated, almost verbatim, seconds later by Lovell. The line seems first to have been used, out of its space-flight context, in print in 1995, the year the film was released, and since then has covered everything from bad comedy shows to, inevitably, the downs in the career of the late soul singer Whitney Houston. It lends itself to puns – Londoners are fond of 'Euston, we have a problem,' in reference to one of the city's main railway stations, and in December 2006, in an article about Nintendo's gaming console, *The New York Times* ran the headline 'Wii have a problem'. The calm, laconic understatement of men facing what must have seemed almost certain to be a lonely death more than 200,000 miles from earth deserves greater respect, for had they and Houston failed in their efforts to bring them safely home, the phrase would now be found only in history books and dictionaries of quotations.

IF YOU CAN REMEMBER [THE SIXTIES *ETC.*] YOU WEREN'T THERE

This over-quoted phrase has been attributed to a number of people; according to *The New York Times* of 7 February 1988 it was coined by the actor and comedian Robin Williams. It probably originated in the 1980s, and is thought to arise from the joke that everyone in the sixties was so stoned they'd have been unaware of what was going on. The phrase was no doubt designed merely to raise a few laughs and then be forgotten. It could even have been meant ironically, for that decade was full of memorable events – the Vietnam War, four assassinations in the US (President Kennedy, Martin Luther King, Malcolm X and Robert Kennedy), the rise of The Beatles, Flower Power, the first two manned moon landings . . . Yet somehow a flippant remark has become a cliché – not only quoted all too often, but adapted to the even more inane 'If you were there in the eighties/the nineties . . .' Maybe there is no limit to how much rubbish people can utter.

IF YOU'VE GOT IT, FLAUNT IT

A slight misquotation of a line from Mel Brooks's 1968 film *The Producers*, in which the theatrical producer and con artist Max Bialystock (Zero Mostel) says: 'That's it, baby, when you got it, flaunt it! Flaunt it!' A variant – 'When you got it, flaunt it!' was an advertising slogan for Braniff Airways from the late 1960s to the mid-1970s, and this probably accounts for the growth of the phrase's popularity. It means if you have something – wealth, good looks, knowledge, some special talent – you should make sure that everyone knows about it. Which is fair enough as far as it goes, for to have a talent and not to use it would be to waste it; however, the expression is often deployed by show-offs as a fairly unsubtle attempt to assert their own smug sense of superiority and to make others envious, which is rather less attractive. In the TV adaptation of one of Ruth Rendell's Inspector Wexford Mysteries, *Simisola*, a character, says: 'What's the use of having money if you don't flaunt it?' The phrase has become hackneyed, and appears in some strange contexts, such as an academic paper for New Mexico State University entitled 'If You Have It, Flaunt It: Using Full Ontological Knowledge for Word Sense Disambiguation', which was probably not what Max Bialystock had in mind. Incidentally, Braniff Airways went bankrupt in May 1982, and according to at least one critic, *The Producers* also records the first use of the term 'creative accounting'(*see* **Blackbox/creative accounting**).

I HEAR YOU/WHAT YOU SAY

A comparatively recent and very annoying phrase that is used far too often. Of course the speaker heard what you've just said; what's more, he has understood or thinks he has understood what you mean. And does not agree with it. The speaker, it is implied, having acknowledged that he has heard you, is going to ignore what you've said as it does not agree with his own opinion. And that's that – debate over.

I know/see where you're coming from

More words that have elbowed themselves from the public-relations and marketing dark side into popular discourse in the 1990s. The tone can be as dismissive as it is in **I hear what you say** – and mean much the same thing – or it can drip with insincerity and be intended to show that the speaker understands completely what you are saying, and why, and will of course bear in mind what you have said . . . Occasionally, it might mean 'I will consider your ideas, could even adopt them as my own' – but more often it means that the speaker is not sure what you're talking about, is not interested, and doesn't agree with you anyway, but will patronize you just in case . . . The riposte has to be: 'And I know where I'm going.'

I'M LOVIN' IT

That rare thing, a catchphrase from an advertisement that we don't owe to Madison Avenue (or at least, not literally; *see also* **'Because I'm worth it'**). In 2003 the ad agency Heye & Partner which, though part of the New York-based global conglomerate Omnicom Group, is based in Germany, beat thirteen other agencies when it came up with 'I'm lovin' it' for the McDonald's Corporation. The world's largest hamburger dispenser was concerned that it was no longer loved. Some unkind people had suggested that it hadn't been loved all that much in the first place, and the year before profits had plunged worldwide. Thanks to the ad – well, 'international branding campaign' – with its accompanying song of the same title performed by Justin Timberlake, sales went up. To be fair to Heye and McDonald's, it is not their fault that the hugely successful slogan should have become a catchphrase, regularly trotted out by celebrities in interviews, and even by politicians in their lighter, man-of-the-people moments. But it has become an irritant, often used without irony to say 'It's good' or 'I like it.' Yet still it goes on, relentlessly, and still no one knows just what 'it' is.

I'M NOT MAKING THIS UP

British talk radio, enabling the masses to speak, live, via phone-ins, was born in the late 1960s. Before then the idea of the people being unleashed to broadcast blasphemy, foul language and inflammatory opinions to each other, unless they were Oxbridge graduates, as the comedian Frankie Howerd pointed out, was unacceptable. In the 1970s, commercial stations were born, and phone-ins were admirably cheap – with enthusiastic listeners volunteering such information as 'I'm a first-time caller' and questions like 'How are you doing?' American talk radio was a 1940s creation, and, particularly after the late-1980s abandonment of regulations, rabid opinions were, on balance, the norm. Thus was it necessary – in order to prod listeners first into existence, then into life, and finally into significant audience ratings – for the freakish, the odd, the different and the bizarre to be promoted as part of the threat to decent folk. The phenomenon spread in a weakened form to Britain, and with it the oft-repeated, and now parodied phrase, perhaps best reinterpreted as 'I am saying this to boost advertising. It also fills in time before death.'

IN THE LOOP

An office cliché which simply means being kept informed about what is going on. It is thought to have originated in the US and is generally believed to derive from computing or electronics, though it could equally come from a loop's resemblance to a circle. The term first appeared in print in *The Sunday Telegraph* as early as 1970: 'Fully automatic landing has now been perfected, though it will still be necessary to keep the pilot "in the loop",' but did not spread until the 1980s; in January 1981 *The New York Times Magazine* remarked, 'The people at the power center have already adopted the White House favorites – "in the loop" for those privileged to be "copied" by receiving copies of memoranda . . .' So an aura of privilege has been conferred upon the term, suggesting that you are a member of the inner circle, privy to important information, and play a vital part in the group or organization – or 'power centre'. In reality, it probably just means that you get sent more memos and e-mails than you want, and are expected to show up at pointless meetings. By extension, you are 'out of the loop' if you are excluded, either intentionally or unintentionally, from a group or process, or have not been kept fully informed of the latest developments within the company, or about who is doing what to whom. This could be because you have been away on holiday – or it could be that they want to get rid of you: it is a fine paranoia-inducing phrase, just as 'in the loop' will feed someone's sense of self-importance.

IT AIN'T OVER TILL IT'S OVER

It was US baseball star and later manager Lawrence Peter 'Yogi' Berra who coined the phrase in 1973. He was then coach of the New York Mets and, halfway through the season, his team was bottom of its division. Asked by the press if the season was finished, he offered 'It ain't over, till it's over' in all its tautological majesty. The Mets went on to top the division. Since then, his words have been used in all areas of life to inspire effort, faith, confidence, support and, just occasionally, caution (it was the title for an episode of the TV series *Hill Street Blues* in May 1987, for instance). On 1 December 2011 the Republican presidential candidate, Herman Cain, assured supporters in New Hampshire it 'ain't over till it's over'. Most of all, however, the phrase is popular as an article headline: Alastair Cooke in his *Letter from America* of 15 February 1999, wrote: 'goings-on [the aftermath of the Clinton-Lewinsky scandal] in the Senate of the United States aren't over till they're over'; *The Daily*

Telegraph headlined an article in November 2009: 'B[ank] o[f] E[ngland]: It ain't over till it's over'; and in November 2011, Guild Investment Management Inc.'s online commentary headlined an article on the financial crisis 'It Ain't Over Till It's Over . . . And That's Not Happening Soon'. To boost the phrase's cliché status, two songs have used it as titles, one by Lenny Kravitz in 1991, and one by DJ Khaled in 2011. As Berra said, on another occasion, 'It's déjà vu all over again'. Incidentally, the subtitle of his *The Yogi Book* (1998) is 'I really didn't say everything I said.'

IT'S NOT ROCKET SCIENCE/
BRAIN SURGERY

No, of course it isn't, so why state the obvious? Why not just say 'It is not that difficult to understand [or 'accomplish']?' which is generally what is meant. Use of the expression might, of course, be worrying if applied to the calculations involved in working out the trajectory of a spacecraft, or to the skills required for operating on the cerebellum, but it never is. One writer of our acquaintance habitually subverts the cliché by saying 'It's not rocket surgery'; he says that it is remarkable how few people notice his small rebellion against the use of this thoroughly timeworn phrase. It is a relatively recent addition to the language – the *Chicago Tribune* of October 1986 is credited with the first printed use of the phrase in this jocular sense – but its overuse has long outweighed its amusement value.

JOINED-UP THINKING

One of those buzz-phrases picked up by politicians, this began life in the mid-1990s, and is only just beginning to make its way to the United States. Originally applied to handwriting – small children print, bigger children and (most) adults 'do joined-up writing' – sometime in the 1980s it was humorously applied to intellectual capacity, making its first known appearance in print in an article in 'the Bible of British adland', *Campaign* magazine, in March 1989, which lamented, 'To our surprise and disappointment, few could manage any joined-up thinking.' Any ironical tone in its everyday use was lost on the British government when it adopted the phrase to mean, roughly, having all departments communicating and acting together purposefully and effectively, and to the good of all. On 4 May 1997 *The Observer* commented, 'The gladiatorial style of debate may give way to what one new woman MP described as "joined-up thinking".' This was with the advent of Tony Blair's 'New' Labour government, but somewhere along the line joined-up thinking was lost: why had obesity rates soared by 2004? Because of a lack of 'joined-up thinking' by the government, said a Parliamentary Select Committee on Health. Why was Britain 'broken' by 2008? 'A lack of joined-up thinking . . .' explained TV host Noel Edmonds. The phrase has been overdone, to the point of meaninglessness, so that besides 'joined-up government', we now have to endure 'joined-up planning', 'joined-up design' and even 'joined-up cooking'.

Kafkaesque

A word that is used by more people than have actually read the works of Franz Kafka. A Czech writer of the early twentieth century, Kafka wrote about a nightmare world in which isolated and distressed characters, intimidated by complex, illogical, impersonal authority, face circumstances that are senseless, surreal and menacing, and by the 1940s his work was seen as a metaphor for incomprehensible, impersonal, labyrinthine and inimical administrative situations. The earliest known appearance in print of 'Kafkaesque' was in *The New Yorker* in January 1947: 'Warned, he said, by a Kafka-esque nightmare of blind alleys.' In January 1972 *Newsweek* referred to 'The Kafkaesque self-abnegation of the infamous "show trials"' in Soviet Russia. Repeated use has, as is always the case, diminished the sense of threat and horror conveyed by the term. *The Guardian* of February 2011 refers to 'A Kafkaesque new system, supposed to make it easier for younger family members to act for elderly relatives, has triggered widespread confusion leading to delays, frustrations and unpaid bills.' Upsetting, confusing, convoluted, annoying – yes; but surely there is not the sense of some unseen terror lurking round the corner? *See also* **Orwellian nightmare**.

KEEP/LEAVE ALL OPTIONS OPEN

An option is a choice, which, if left undecided upon, is 'open' – a relatively recent construction, according to *The Guardian* of 14 May 1969: 'Mr Callaghan . . . is understood to have reserved his decision – or, in the current jargon, "kept his options open".' Occasionally, options are left 'on the table' (where as long ago as the seventeenth century, reports, bills or proposals would be left for further consideration). Keeping (or leaving) options open usually means putting off making a decision – more time is needed to consider the options, the person is anxious not to rule anything out just yet, wants to stay flexible – or is hoping that a new, more attractive option will present itself. In politics and business, especially, keeping options open is often a popular strategy. Donald Trump, nursing hopes of getting into the presidential race, announced in December 2011: 'I must leave all of my options open because, above all else, we must make America great again!' (which is a magnificent non sequitur, as well). Meanwhile, the current president is not committing himself to attacking Iran in support of Israel, saying he is 'leaving all options on the table' (*The Economist*, February 2012). 'Keeping our options open' – it seems sensible, doesn't it? Almost irresistible. But it has been argued that keeping your options open can lose you motivation, money and time, while it might indicate to others a lack of commitment, even reliability.

KICK ASS, TO / KICK-ASS

The ass, that domesticated hoofed mammal (as the *OED* calls it) is, of course, not the subject of discussion here. Instead it is the American for the ancient (like, tenth-century) British 'arse', which provides a starting point, after which the debate meanders. Can we handle so much kick-assing? It may be that a person, or object, is indeed awesome. Right? It may also be that, in the wake of an unforeseen setback, such as that suffered by Australian tennis player Pat Cash, after losing at Wimbledon in 1988 he just wanted to 'go out and kick ass' – behaving in an aggressive manner, raging against the fates. You may have attained a level of competence deserving respect, as described by American singer Nicole Scherzinger, telling *The Daily Mirror* in 2011 about life with British racing driver Lewis Hamilton. 'If I wanna go crazy I'll have a game night', she explained. 'We play Cranium, Taboo or cards. I can kick ass but Lewis is pretty good at cards. He's pretty good at everything.'

Knee-jerk reaction

'Knee jerk' was introduced into the language in the 1870s to describe the involuntary movement of the leg that results from a sharp tap on the patellar tendon, otherwise known as 'checking the reflexes'. By the 1960s, the term 'knee-jerk' was being applied to American liberals in particular: 'The place has always been full of liberals . . . In Washington, we call them crack-pots, knee-jerks, do-gooders' (*New York Times* 7 October 1963). Then came 'knee-jerk reaction' to describe an immediate, unthinking, emotional response to an event or statement. Today, almost every response to an event seems to be labelled by the press 'knee-jerk', particularly if these responses are political efforts to show the world that Something is Being Done: in June 2010 the British Prime Minister David Cameron said 'there should not be a "knee-jerk reaction" to changing the laws on gun ownership after twelve people were shot dead in Cumbria,' according to BBC News, but little more than a year later his bid to evict rioters from their council homes was branded a 'knee-jerk reaction'; 'Israeli officials warn of "knee-jerk" showdown with Iran,' reads a February 2012 headline in *USA Today*; the US 'war on terror' has been described as 'the longest-ever knee-jerk reaction'. Haven't we had enough of all these legs waving about?

LEARNING CURVE

We owe this term to the German psychologist Hermann Ebbinghaus who, in 1885, found that the time required to memorize a nonsense word increased sharply as the number of syllables increased. (Ebbinghaus also studied the 'forgetting curve' although, unsurprisingly, that is a less popular concept.) The rate of learning (first of rats, then children as their development was researched by educationalists and psychologists) was measured using a simple graph – the horizontal axis representing time, the vertical axis the amount learned. The steeper the curve, the faster the subject was learning. The term was being used in business as early as 1968: *Management Glossary*, edited by Hano Johannsen and Andrew Robertson, explaining that 'Learning curves indicate how the rate of learning changes with increased practice.' During the rest of the twentieth century the term spread through industry, business and commerce, nearly always preceded by the adjective 'steep', used to announce that those employing the phrase are in the business of learning a great deal very quickly – or to remind new employees that much is expected from them and they won't be given any time in which to learn it. It is not surprising, therefore, that 'steep learning curve' is often wrongly used to refer to the difficulty of learning something. So if you want to use the term correctly, avoid the cliché.

LET ME BE ABSOLUTELY CLEAR

An absolutely popular response among those handling the absolutely complex issue of clearness in absolutely awkward situations. In 2008 presidential candidate Barack Obama visited Israel, and told Israelis, 'Let me be absolutely clear, Israel is a strong friend of Israel's.' While that was absolutely true, Obama had *wished* to be absolutely clear by saying 'the United States'. This did nothing to deter him from using his favourite opening phrase again and again, suggesting as it does both open honesty and firmness. 'Let me be absolutely clear here: I opposed this war in 2002. I opposed it in 2003, '04, '05, '06 and '07,' he said in March 2008; and in April 2011: 'Let me be absolutely clear: I will preserve these health-care programmes . . .' It has caught on, even the opposition adopting it: 'Let me be absolutely clear,' declared failed presidential candidate Michele Bachmann on 1 February 2012, 'there are absolutely no negotiations between me and the Romney campaign regarding any pending endorsement of Governor Romney.' Meanwhile, across the Atlantic, the prime minister, David Cameron, had assured Parliament in January 2011: 'Let me be absolutely clear, phone hacking is wrong and illegal.' Eleven months later, he promised the Falkland Islanders: 'So let me be absolutely clear. We will always maintain our commitment to you on any question of sovereignty . . .' So now we know it: politicians like to be clear. Absolutely clear.

LEVEL PLAYING FIELD

Just how level is a playing field? 'The city school board is having a sports field developed in the rear of George Washington High School . . . The city engineer has drafted the plans for the removal of dirt so as to afford a level playing field,' *The Bee* (Danville, Virginia), September 1927. Today, the phrase is better known as a metaphor – even, ludicrously, when referring to a sport: 'In polo, better players "give away" goals to their weaker opponents to create a level playing field for a match,' wrote the *Deccan Herald* (Bangalore, India) as early as January 1953. It was only in the 1970s, however, that the expression established itself, first of all in the USA, to mean that everyone would have the same opportunities and advantages and would play by the same set of rules; all would be fair and everything would be lovely. Oft-repeated, so well known has the phrase become that it has given its name to an organization, the Level Playing Field Institute, in San Francisco, which devotes itself to creating 'a world where a true level playing field exists'. Sadly, the world is not fair – those who talk of level playing fields usually mean 'playing fields' that are advantageous to them, never mind other people.

LICENCE TO PRINT MONEY

This expression is believed to have been coined by the Canadian newspaper proprietor Roy Thomson, later Lord Thomson of Fleet, who bought the commercial TV franchise Scottish Television in 1957, later remarking that it was 'like having your own licence to print money'. An enviable position indeed, and it was greatly envied. Possibly used more in the UK, the expression was nevertheless adopted early in the USA, with *Time* magazine printing an article in November 1969 about American Express's business ventures under the heading 'Corporations: A License to Print Money'. Over the years the phrase has become a favourite complaint about any venture that appears to be raking in money while making no visible effort, generally to the detriment of the person using the phrase. Internet-service provider not delivering the broadband widths it promised you? 'Licence to print money, isn't it?' Speeding fines and parking charges? 'A licence to print money . . .' The rise in the cost of fuel, of cigarettes, alcohol . . . all licences to print money. And so on, as an original comment becomes a tired cliché.

LOL

Born of Internet chatspeak (apparently first used on Usenet in the 1980s) and now used copiously in text messaging and social networking (unfortunately, it is escaping those boundaries, and has even entered speech, pronounced 'loll'). In the 1960s, LOL stood for 'little old lady', usually applied to the indomitable type of old lady, but it is only rarely used nowadays. Today, it can mean 'lots of love' or 'lots of luck', but its main (and original Usenet) meaning is 'laugh(ing) out loud'. The likelihood that anyone is laughing out loud, or laughing at all, is slim, but the term seems to be used to acknowledge that whatever they are responding to was funny, or that the story they have just told should be seen as funny rather than as a calamity ('I fell and cracked my skull. LOL').

Quite apart from its overuse, anyone who wishes to send lots of love should take care; a message reading 'Sorry to hear of your heart attack. LOL' might well be misinterpreted, and cause offence. Or another heart attack . . .

MINDSET

A psychologists' term that has been adopted into office and everyday language, where its meaning has grown woollier. 'Habits of mind formed by previous events or earlier environment which affect a person's attitude,' expounds the *OED* grandiosely, while the *American Heritage Dictionary* explains that a mindset is 'A fixed mental attitude or disposition that predetermines a person's responses to and interpretations of situations.' One definition looking to the past, the other looking ahead: it is no wonder that the phrase is used to mean whatever those using it think they want to say. The British footballer Graeme Le Saux said in an interview in June 2005: 'I've never put myself in the mindset that I'm actually any good at taking pictures, I just love to shoot things that catch my eye, whether it's landscapes or just my kids.' What he meant was that he didn't believe he was that good at taking pictures – and he might wish he had worded the last part of his sentence differently. Kevin Mitnick, an American computer-security consultant and former hacker, told an interviewer in April 2004 that 'The hacker mindset doesn't actually see what happens on the other side, to the victim.' Mindsets can *see*? But then, according to the Nobel Prize-winning economist Muhammad Yunus, 'Mindsets play strange tricks on us.' In context, however, he is making perfect sense, referring to the dyed-in-the-wool attitudes of the bankers who refused to believe that the poor villagers of Bangladesh could be credit-worthy: 'We see things the way our minds have instructed our eyes to see.' (He was right.) As with so many clichés, a word that once had a defined meaning in a particular field has become almost worthless, little more than a pompous way of saying 'outlook' or 'attitude'.

Move the goalposts

To make an arbitrary and unfair change in the rules of a situation or negotiation, especially to make it harder for someone to achieve something. The metaphor's derivation from games that use goalposts is obvious; its country of origin is less clear: Sir Peter Stothard, then US editor of *The Times*, said in the 1980s that the term is British and probably from children's games, where easily moved sticks or discarded coats are used as goalposts. The earliest recorded mention in print, however, was in *The Washington Post* in 1978 quoting American Airlines' CEO's reaction to deregulation: '"They keep moving the goal posts," he lamented.' The first British reference in print seems to have come from the Chancellor of the Exchequer Nigel Lawson, quoted in the Jamaican newspaper *The Gleaner* of September 1987 as saying 'I see no reason to move the goalposts at all.' In 1990 President Bush remarked 'I do not believe in moving the goalposts,' while in July 2011, House Speaker John A. Boehner complained that 'the White House moved the goalpost'. In commerce and elsewhere, as in politics, there are accusations of goalposts being moved – big businesses and financial corporations are always moving goalposts . . . Office managers move goalposts, as do teachers and parents: the phrase has become so worn out that it was refreshing when the Danish goalkeeper Kim Christensen literally moved the goalposts during a 2009 football match, and admitted to the press having done so 'from time to time'.

MOVERS AND SHAKERS

People, usually prominent in their fields, who get things done, shape events, help form opinions – in other words, people of power and influence. The term was coined by a little-known Victorian poet named Arthur O'Shaughnessy, whose 'Ode' of 1874 contains the lines: 'We are the movers and shakers / Of the world for ever, it seems.' Which is ironic, since O'Shaughnessy's movers and shakers were 'the music makers . . . the dreamers of dreams . . . world-losers and world-forsakers,' not the rich and powerful in politics and business. But his poetic phrase has become a favourite of journalists, especially when describing those attending such events as the annual World Economic Forum in Davos, Switzerland. It became common in American usage from the 1960s – the online Phrase Finder cites a reference in *Ebony* magazine of July 1962 – and had crossed the Atlantic by the next decade, although by then few who used it were aware of its poetic origins. Away from world affairs, business and the media, however, it has become overused, and inevitably weaker as a result. It is fair enough to use it of, say, the big cheeses in the oil industry or the music business, but to talk of 'the movers and shakers of the beekeeping world' is carrying bathos too far. But in truth, like **blood and treasure**, its slightly self-conscious old-fashionedness suggests that it is time it was retired.

MULTI-TASK

Another escapee from computing and not, as might be thought, from the women's liberation movement. It dates from the mid-1960s, in reference to computers that could perform two or more functions concurrently. Nowadays, when a single smartphone has far more processing power than the computers that sent *Apollo 11* to the moon and back, this doesn't seem much of a trick, but it was a considerable advance back then. By 1983 *The Times* was predicting the arrival of 'multi-task work stations . . . for one in six offices within five to ten years', and two years later the Apricot Xen PC was advertised as allowing 'you to multi-task, doing your word-processing while your Apricot simultaneously busies itself with your accounts'. Today, however, the phrase is as likely as not to be used in business of people who are able to do more than one task at a time, and especially of women, who are widely believed to be better at multi-tasking (or 'multitasking') than men. As a result, it has lost definition, and become just a cliché for someone who's good at juggling tasks in the workplace and at home. People who consider themselves good at multi-tasking might care to reflect on an older English cliché: 'Jack of all trades and master of none'.

New —, The (*as in* 'Red is the new black') – *see* X is the new Y

No pain, no gain

A take on the old maxim that nothing is won without effort, this phrase gained currency in the early 1980s, as an encouraging motto for people doing fitness exercises; it was a favourite of Jane Fonda's in her aerobics videos. It is little more than a variant of the now declining cliché 'Nothing ventured, nothing gained,' a version of which was used by Chaucer in the fourteenth century, but its ancestry is as distinguished. The English poet Robert Herrick added a couplet to the 1650 edition of his collection *Hesperides* headed 'No pains, no gains,' and in 1734 Benjamin Franklin, under his pseudonym 'Poor Richard', wrote: 'He that lives upon hope will die fasting. There are no gains, without pains.' It is acceptable to use the phrase, hackneyed as it is, of an exercise routine, and even of some beneficial, if unpleasant, treatment such as root-canal work. It is much less so, however, when it is deployed by politicians of some new 'austerity' programme, largely because the pain is unlikely to afflict them. Besides, on the whole it seems reasonable to suggest that a better motto may be 'No pain, no pain'.

Not an option, [Something] is

Most commonly heard as 'Failure is not an option,' possibly because the line was written for Ed Harris's portrayal of Gene Kranz, NASA's Flight Director for the Apollo 13 space mission of April 1970, in the film *Apollo 13* (1995). In fact, Kranz, who played a crucial role in the rescue, denied that he had ever said this, although he did use the phrase for the title of his autobiography, which appeared in 2000. (*See also* **'Houston, we have a problem'**.) It has become a rather laboured and pompous way of saying that something must be done or has to be made to succeed, often with a slightly threatening ring to it: 'In your case, Robinson, overspend on this project is not an option.' It has been thoroughly overworked, partly because politicians like to deploy it, and it is also favoured by the self-help industry: 'Giving up is not an option!' For the benefit of clear speech, using it to mean 'We have to avoid such-and-such an outcome' should not be – well – an option.

OMG!

A phrase that originated, round about 1994, in online chat and transferred to text-message shorthand ('textspeak') and e-mail, it has now spread into the language itself. It stands for 'Oh my God!' (or sometimes 'Oh my goodness!' or 'Oh my gosh!') and, away from text-messaging, is often written 'Omigod!' The online Urban Dictionary describes it as: 'Possibly the most irritating piece of chatroom vernacular in existence. Often used by teenage girls in chatroom[s] who, for some reason, punctuate their sentences with "Like", "Totally", "Sooooo" and "Lolz"' (the last is the plural of **LOL**. Apparently). It cannot be stopped; only the advance of technology, or its users' sudden recognition that it is vacuous as well as worn-out, will drive it from usage.

ON-[*OR* OFF-] MESSAGE

Both on-message and its slightly later sibling, 'off-message', owe their existence to journalists' comments about the then soon-to-be US President Clinton in the early 1990s. The phrase is useful shorthand for 'toeing the party line' or 'following company policy'; just as its antonym, 'off-message', is for (sometimes deliberately) not doing so. As often as not nowadays it is used only to mean can someone be trusted to do what his or her seniors expect or demand, when it is just a hackneyed euphemism for 'loyal', 'dependable' or 'obedient'. Problems also arise when it is not clear what message the person is on, or meant to be on, as in a headline from *The Washington Times* in February 2012: 'Obama stays on "message", gets boost in ratings amid GOP strife.' Surely President Obama *is* the message, so why would he stray from it? Finally, a warning: one man's on-message person may be another's sycophant or toady – ass-kisser, in the vernacular. The much earlier (1912) US term 'yes-man' (or '-woman', or '-girl') springs to mind.

'(THAT'S) ONE SMALL STEP FOR MAN, . . .'

'. . . One giant leap for mankind,' said Neil Armstrong as he stepped on to the moon's surface on 21 July 1969, the first human being ever to do so (well, so far as we know).

The American astronaut has always maintained that he had said 'a man', but it was undeniably, and rightly, a step – and a soundbite – that has gone into the history books. Unfortunately, it has also been poached for articles about and advertisements for everything from education policy to bicycles, the two phrases often separated, so that 'One small step' may be promoting a British bank, while 'One giant leap' is being used as the title for a feature-length documentary featuring the 'concept band and media project' 1 Giant Leap. It is sometimes the fate of quotations that have become justifiably famous that they will in time become clichés; Winston Churchill's 'This was their finest hour' and John F. Kennedy's 'Ask not what your country can do for you' being but two examples. When you hear someone say 'Our new software package is one giant leap for . . .' you know that it's time to retire the phrase.

ONE-TRICK PONY

A phrase from the circus, where a performing animal that could manage more than one trick was bound to be a bigger crowd-puller than its less talented fellows. It is American in origin and dates from the early years of the twentieth century, and was often applied disparagingly to the small travelling circuses which, having no major acts or wild animals such as tigers and elephants, came to be known as 'dog-and-pony shows'; clearly such a show would be even poorer if the ponies could only manage a single trick. By the late 1980s it was being applied in American business to any person, object or proposal that had only a single special talent, expertise or feature. It is probably dying out, having been flogged to death (as many trick ponies were in circuses before animal-rights legislation caught up with them) as a pejorative way of slightly disparaging someone or something. Its use is often thoughtlessly inane, as in 'The new coffee machine is a bit of a one-trick pony.' What else did the speaker expect the machine to do, other than dispense coffee? Sit up and beg?

ORWELLIAN NIGHTMARE

It is a particular kind of fame for a writer to find his name turned into an adjective, and just that befell the English novelist, essayist and journalist George Orwell (born Eric Arthur Blair; 1903-50). His literary and journalistic output included few chortle-inducing rib-ticklers, but the work was enormously rich and varied. It culminated in the volumes that led to the phrase that has fed headline-writers and hacks looking to beef up the banal ever since (the first printed use of 'Orwellian' dates from the year of his death, 1950, in a piece by Mary McCarthy). *Animal Farm* (1945) was a satire on the Soviet Union's degeneration into Joseph Stalin's dictatorship, and *1984* (1949, but written in 1948) was a vision of an endless totalitarian world, and 'a boot stamping on a human face – for ever'. There are, however, other kinds of nightmare, and other adjectives with which to describe them. To say that paying a parking fine proved to be an 'Orwellian nightmare' is not only carrying hyperbole too far, but also debases the meaning of the useful adjective 'Orwellian'. *See also* **Kafkaesque**.

PARADIGM SHIFT

Originally a term describing a fundamental change in scientific theory, the phrase was coined by the American science historian and philosopher Thomas Kuhn in his *The Structure of Scientific Revolutions* (1962). It means, in other words, a change so profound and far-reaching that it alters world-views. Given that simplicity and precision of language are the greatest aids to being understood, it is worrying to find no less than the chairman of the Scottish White Fish Producers' Association noting in 2011, 'a paradigm shift in the way we manage fisheries' and, in March the same year, a *New York Times* journalist observing that 'after lying in a fur hammock for about forty seconds, a paradigm shift takes place.' In general use, the phrase is just a lazy and long-winded way of suggesting little more than a new plan or a different way of looking at something, a sad end for 'paradigm', which first appeared in print in the fifteenth century, in William Caxton's translation and printing of the *Golden Legend* of Jacobus de Voragine.

PARAMETER

A word that originated in mathematics during the seventeenth century, 'parameter' is one of those terms with a highly technical meaning – several, in fact – that has been largely lost through its misuse in general applications. This seems to have started in the late 1950s and gained in popularity; this is from an article in *The New York Times Magazine* of February 1973: 'It carries, to begin with, the liberal presumption that the mind of man can in fact comprehend the major parameters of the world we inhabit.' Properly, a parameter is not a limit or a boundary, nor a distinguishing characteristic or feature, nor a factor, although that is how it is often used. It has a number of specific meanings in the fields of mathematics, physics, statistics, astronomy, and so on – look up 'Racah parameters', for instance, which will take you into the world of quantum mechanics – and as such is best left to those who know how to employ it correctly. As one online dictionary rather loftily puts it, its use to mean 'limiting factor' probably came about 'because of its ring of technical authority'.

PAST ITS SELL-BY DATE

A phrase that is itself now well past its sell-by date, it is used colloquially, mainly in business, for an idea or even a product that is no longer considered attractive, useful, practical, up-to-date, or is in some other way no longer wanted. It comes from the crazy world of stock control, particularly in supermarkets, and the introduction of such dates on the packaging of perishable items in the early 1970s. It refers only to a product's shelf life (it is sometimes seen as a 'display-until' date), and food that is past its sell-by date is not necessarily past its 'use-by date', after which it might become dangerous to eat (or, in the case of medicines, to use). By the late 1980s the phrase had started to be employed metaphorically, as in this heading from *The Daily Telegraph* in March 1987: 'Socialism: the package that's passed its sell-by date.' It is a slightly laboured analogy in any case, and its amusement value has long since evaporated.

People: Get your people to talk to my people

This is people as in 'employees', with a distinct undertone of 'my underlings'. The speaker is both too busy, and too important, to make his or her own arrangements, which must be left to loyal, reliable and efficient, but otherwise insignificant, minions. Anyone thinking of using the expression might want to consider just what a conversation between two such 'people' might sound like:

'Hi, is that A from Consolidated B? This is X from Y Amalgamated.'

'Sure. How can I help?'

'My boss wants me to set up a meeting with your boss.'

'What for? They're both morons.'

'True. But Madam took a bath on that investment scam – y'know, the one about making gold from seawater? – and wants to find out if your guy did too.'

'Sure he did. Bath and a half. Said he didn't, but I've seen the figures.'

'Okay, what say we make 'em meet halfway?'

'Yeah, I like that. How 'bout Gilbert, Arizona, in a couple of months?'

'Done!'

Luckily, the phrase is mainly used ironically, or even self-deprecatingly nowadays, which is just as well, since anyone employing it in all seriousness merits only ridicule.

PEOPLE'S, THE

Arguably, in the sense of being both admired and chosen by the people, a cliché popularized by the former British prime minister Tony Blair, whose reaction to the sudden and tragic death of Diana, Princess of Wales in August 1997 led him to describe her as 'the people's princess'. There had been 'the people's' this and that before then, of course – 'people's champions', 'people's choices' and 'people's voices' have been used of sportsmen, politicians, newspapers, foodstuffs and other products, and much else besides, since at least the mid-nineteenth century – but Blair's shocked and sincere tribute brought the phrase back into common currency. It has been overworked since, however, so that the Duchess of Cambridge – the former Kate Middleton, who married the late Princess's eldest son, Prince William, in April 2011 – has several times been referred to in the press as 'the people's princess', perhaps signifying a lapse in journalistic imagination, and at the same time irritating all those who feel that Diana's memory should be kept inviolate. Meanwhile, you can find advertisements for everything from 'the People's Supermarket' to *The People's Friend*, the British story magazine first published in 1869, or you can vote in the People's Choice Awards which annually reward the 'people and the work of popular culture' (i.e. Hollywood, mainly), or, in Britain, sign up for the People's Charter. And there's always the People's Republic of China . . . Time to abandon the phrase, unless something genuinely is of, by and for the people.

PLAN B

What you adopt once Plan A has failed, or propose in case Plan A should fail. By a charming quirk of lexicography, the earliest printed reference to Plan B, in a letter from the US Civil War in 1863, predates the earliest citation – again from the USA – for Plan A by seven years. Its colloquial use – 'freq. humorous', as the dictionary puts it – dates from the late 1970s, once more an American usage, though it was established in British English by the late 1980s. Alex Garland's 1997 novel *The Beach* puts it well: 'The only problem with plan B was that, like most plan B's, it didn't exist' (though a purist might object to the apostrophe). It is certainly true that Britain's Chancellor of the Exchequer, the

Conservative George Osborne, has claimed that there is no Plan B where his austerity measures to restore the country's economy are concerned. The problem is that the term is increasingly used simply to mean an alternative proposal or course of action, and has become hackneyed as a result. When *Time* magazine reported in July 2001 that 'For the past 14 years, Yucca has been the only site for a permanent repository in which to store nuclear waste. There is no Plan B,' it made a valid, and perhaps worrying, point. But to say 'If the bar's closed, what's Plan B?' is an example of a kind of slightly laboured jocularity from which the charm has long since vanished.

POISONED CHALICE

'Chalice' is an old-fashioned or poetic word for a goblet or drinking-cup, though it is still used for the vessel in which the wine is offered at Holy Communion. Its first recorded use in English dates from the ninth century, but the expression 'poisoned chalice' dates from the seventeenth century, and specifically Shakespeare's *Macbeth* (1605) which, in Act I, Scene vii, has the lines: 'This even-handed justice / Commends the ingredients of our poison'd chalice / To our own lips.' This is Macbeth's vision of murdering the king by offering him poison in a cup, and over time the phrase has come to mean anything that seems good but which is likely to turn sour or bad, as in 'I suspect her promotion to Head of IT will prove to be a poisoned chalice.' The expression has become a cliché through overuse, compounded by its often being applied inappropriately: something that is merely bad, unpleasant, disappointing, or similar, is not a poisoned chalice.

POLITICAL CORRECTNESS (GONE MAD)

The phrase 'political correctness' dates from late 1940s America, although the term 'politically correct' first appeared in print in the USA in 1793, and was established on both sides of the Atlantic by the mid-1950s. Perhaps as a result of programmes to teach or even enforce political correctness that were introduced in schools, universities, companies, unions, political bodies and other organizations, by the late 1970s both the concept and the phrase were generating a backlash, and would often be seen in conjunction with the adjective 'smug'. The abbreviation 'PC', which first appeared in print in this sense in *The New York Times* in 1986, is often used sardonically or even pejoratively, and never more so than in the construction, beloved of tabloid newspaper headlines, 'Political correctness gone mad!' This is deployed whenever some action or edict is deemed to have overstepped the boundaries of what is reasonable or even sensible, as when – allegedly – 'A school in Seattle renamed its Easter eggs "spring spheres" to avoid causing offence to people who did not celebrate Easter.' It is also true, however, that the phrase is often deployed whenever the commentator happens personally to disagree with some aspect of political correctness, which is not actually proof that PC has gone mad. The phrase has become clichéd to such an extent that it is now most often used sarcastically. In consequence, 'PC-gone-mad' discussions drive all involved, regardless of race, caste, creed, gender persuasion or political outlook, mad.

Proactive

The opposite of 'reactive', meaning to act in advance of something happening, rather than simply reacting to it after the event. It has been a vogue word for years, entering business-speak in the 1980s because it sounds, y'know, kind of thrusting and go-ahead, and a bit technical. The earliest printed reference is from 1933, in a highly specific psychological application; by 1971, however, it was being applied in a looser sense, to mean taking the initiative or anticipating events. (Curiously, several of the *OED*'s citations for this meaning are about policing, causing the late American writer and journalist William Safire, who wrote widely on English usage, to remark, in an article in *The New York Times Magazine* in March 1980, that reactive law enforcement responds after a bank has been robbed, whereas in proactive enforcement the police are in on the planning stages of a crime.) In truth, the word is timeworn to the point at which it is now just another way of saying 'innovative'. That it is much used in job advertisements, résumés, company promotions, and explanations of new political initiatives ought to be enough to consign it to history, other than in specific usage.

PUSHING THE ENVELOPE

It is never a good idea to try to hammer a technical term – in this case, from aeronautics (and, in particular, military aeronautics) – to fit something as banal as, say, next quarter's sales projections, the launch of a new brand, an article about some new development or other, or the latest political initiative. It is a sound rule of English that technical terms are best left to those who know how to use them. The phrase derives from the term 'flight envelope', meaning 'the range of combinations of speed, altitude, angle of attack, etc., within which a flying object is aerodynamically stable'. It became popular, in a general sense of pushing the boundaries of what is possible, after the publication of Tom Wolfe's book about the US space programme, *The Right Stuff*, in 1979 – however, Wolfe was writing about flight testing, the very thing for which the term was coined (the earliest printed reference to the 'flight envelope' is from an aeronautics journal in 1944). So if you hear someone say in a meeting 'We're really pushing the envelope here,' you can be reasonably certain that you are in the presence of someone basking in self-congratulation.

Quantum leap

In physics, a quantum leap (or 'jump', but also sometimes called an 'atomic electron transition') is an abrupt change in the quantum state of an electron, atom or molecule. The use of the phrase in business and journalism to mean a large, even dramatic, advance in something, often leapfrogging transitional stages, is quite a good example of why technical language is best left to people who know how to use it (*see* **Pushing the envelope**). The Soviet Union's successful launching of the first satellite into earth orbit was a quantum leap in the international space race, and if the Large Hadron Collider at the European Organization for Nuclear Research's laboratory, on the French-Swiss border, does indeed discover the Higgs–Boson (or 'God') particle, that will signal a quantum leap in the understanding and study of theoretical physics. A headline on the US sports-media website Bleacher Report, however, reading 'Rojo Remembers: Pole-Vaulting's Quantum Leap,' doesn't carry quite the same weight, somehow. Ironically, quantum leaps occur at sub–microscopic levels, whereas the phrase in common usage indicates something vast. Reasonably, therefore, it should only be used to indicate something of enormous significance, or a truly spectacular and unexpected advance in something.

RAISE THE BAR/ONE'S GAME

When a high-jumper or pole-vaulter clears the bar, it is raised for the next attempt. As a result, 'raising the bar' has come to be used figuratively, especially in business, of decisions to increase the quality, specification, ambitiousness etc. of something, and so exceed expectations. Here is Diane Ravitch, a former US Assistant Secretary of Education: 'If we are going to raise the bar we must take the necessary steps to help students reach it.' Well and good (although surely the ambitious students should clear the bar, rather than just reach it?); however, a statement like 'Adding a cherry to our range of cupcakes has really raised the bar for our competition' manages to be as inane as it is bathetic. Once the bar has been raised, you may need to raise your game. This expression comes from tennis, and refers to a player increasing his or her effort and commitment in order to beat an opponent. By the 1980s it had transferred from sports commentary to political punditry, as in this comment on a US website called Mr. Media Training, of one of the debates between Republican candidates for the presidential nomination in September 2011: 'Sen. Santorum raised his game tonight, and came across with credibility when attacking Gov. Perry.' It is a useful phrase as shorthand for someone who performs better or more effectively, and with increased effort, but it has become hackneyed through overuse or slightly inappropriate applications: 'It was agreed that the Council needed to raise its game over the street-lighting issue.'

RATIONALIZING

A word coined in the early nineteenth century, meaning to make something conform to reason, or to explain something rationally, and with additional meanings in maths, physics and psychology. Unfortunately, however, it seems to have been hijacked in the 1920s to describe organizing or reorganizing a business 'on rational or scientific principles' to meet a particular target or set of targets. In practice, this almost invariably means **downsizing**, the aim usually being to reduce the number of staff, buildings, factories, product lines etc. so that the remainder are deployed more efficiently. In other words, in this usage it is rarely more than business jargon for a reduction in size or numbers, a tired euphemism for 'We are getting rid of a number of staff.'

REAL TERMS, IN

According to one online dictionary, this means 'Growth, income, value, wage, yield etc., expressed as a quantity from which unreal (apparent or nominal) increase caused by inflation has been subtracted.' In other words, it describes money in terms of its actual purchasing power, rather than its nominal or face value. For instance, Oliver Goldsmith's parson in *The Deserted Village* is said to be 'passing rich with forty pounds a year'. That £40 (US $63) today, in real terms, would be unlikely to last him a week. The phrase has been lifted from the world of the economist and adopted in everyday speech, becoming more and more meaningless because it is generally just a filler, perhaps added for emphasis. 'We must take a decision as to what it is we want, in real terms' is a rambling way of saying 'We must decide what we want,' the last three words almost completely meaningless.

REAL TIME

A computing term from the 1950s that has found its way into other industries, notably film and television, as well as marketing-speak. In essence, something that happens in real time happens instantly (there are other technical meanings in the computing world, but these, luckily, fall outside the scope of this book), without delaying constraints – for instance, a computerized guided-missile system must operate in real time. In more general use, a good example is twenty-four-hour rolling news, where events are reported within minutes of their happening, rather than after a delay of perhaps hours while they are assessed and bulletins prepared. The problem with the phrase – which many people use because they think it sounds impressive, **cutting edge**, up to the minute – is that it has different shades of meaning beyond its technical usage. So a movie or TV drama in real time is one in which the action occupies exactly the time the programme lasts, a good example being the Fox Network series *24*, in which twenty-four episodes covered twenty-four hours in Jack Bauer's life. Slightly lower down the scale of usefulness, 'real–time marketing' is designed to respond quickly to the dictates of the target market. Less helpfully still, a 'real–time meeting' is one in which the participants meet face to face, without the delays of, say, correspondence. Since it is not (yet) possible to hold such a meeting other than in real time, its use here is plain silly, as well as confusing and unnecessary.

REINVENTING THE WHEEL

At its most basic, this means what a Victorian might have described as 'work of supererogation' – that is, doing more than is required. Wikipedia describes the phrase as an 'idiomatic metaphor', but in almost all political, journalistic, advertising and business applications, it is a cliché, and not a particularly helpful one, at that. The *OED* dates the first printed reference to an advertisement in *The Times* in January 1967, which means that it has had forty-five years in which to become thoroughly worn out. The expression, which is undeniably colourful, properly means to recreate something that already exists, but is now mainly used to mean repeating a task unnecessarily. A reinvention of the wheel would be a hugely significant event in human history, whereas duplication of effort in business or government is so common as to be ordinary. The phrase is used, more technically, in higher education and in computer programming – and if you really want to be obscure, you can talk about its close relations, 'preinventing the wheel' and 'reinventing the square wheel'. Perhaps not, on reflection.

REVOLVING-DOOR POLICY

The first patent for a revolving door was granted to a German inventor in Berlin in 1881, but it was the Philadelphian Theodore van Kannel whose 1888 US patent really put the device on the map. Being draught-free, the doors were quickly taken up by the likes of banks, hotels and department stores, and many are still in use today. The name was also a gift as a metaphor, so that by 1914 *The Atlanta Constitution* was reporting, of the Mexican politician Félix Díaz, that he wanted 'somebody else to push the revolving door of revolution around for him'. In business, it quickly came to mean a company's tendency to change personnel regularly, but in politics it tends to be used of senior figures who leave government employment for jobs in industry (for which read 'extremely well-rewarded jobs'). But it has also broadened to mean any, perhaps rather unenviable, job which has a high turnover of occupants. Thus a sports report in *The Washington Post* of March 2003: 'He could provide some stability at kicker, a position that has been a revolving door for years.' Since the meaning of the phrase is often at best unclear, it is hardly a useful addition to the language.

RIGHT-THINKING (*OR* RIGHT-MINDED) PEOPLE

Not, perhaps surprisingly, people of the political Right, but people who hold sound or acceptable views or principles, sometimes themselves known as 'right-thinkers'. The phrase, which first appeared in print in 1829, is a variant of the older term 'right-minded' – 'having a mind naturally inclined or disposed towards what is right' – which is how it usually appears in the USA. It is much employed by politicians, typically in appealing to 'right-thinking people everywhere', in which form it has become a cliché. It has an especial weasel quality, though, in that the speaker very often doesn't actually mean right-thinking people, but people who agree with him or her, which is not necessarily – perhaps not even often – the same thing. It is interesting to note that in

America, 'right-minded' conservative moms (among other groups) frequently speak out against Sarah Palin – who is, of course, Right-minded.

RING-FENCE

Dating from the late eighteenth century, as a noun this originally meant a fence entirely enclosing an estate or other property. It is legal language, and within a hundred years was being used metaphorically to mean a barrier set in place to protect or preserve something. Of British origin, it is slowly making its way across the Atlantic, one commentator in the USA suggesting that the 2010 Gulf of Mexico oil spill might be ring-fenced with floating barriers, a literal use of the term (*see also* **Better late than never**). After the worldwide recession took hold in 2008 the phrase became a favourite of politicians, notably in ring-fencing a budget to keep it safe from the massive cuts they saw as needed to restore financial equilibrium. But it is in the financial world that the phrase is most often encountered, as when a company may ring-fence its bad assets to preserve its good ones, or investors ring-fence certain funds to keep them from the tax man. In the present climate, bankers ring-fencing their bonuses would probably be seen as a bad move,

PR–wise. It is a poor term to use when all that is meant is 'protect' or 'preserve', as in 'I want to ring-fence the weekly meeting before they try to make it monthly.'

ROFL

Text-message chatspeak, meaning 'I am convulsed with amusement upon hearing this news,' or 'Rolling On [the] Floor Laughing'; true texting devotees may even use 'ROFLOL', for 'rolling on floor laughing out loud'. Like other textspeak (*see* **LOL**; **OMG**), it came about because it is impossible to see or hear a person's reaction to a text message. It has become tiresome, however, because it is so often misused, someone sending 'ROFL' when in fact what they mean is 'That's mildly amusing,' or 'It made me smile.' In speech it is pronounced 'roffle' – which is a bit strange, as why would you say it to someone when, by your own account, you are rolling on the floor, laughing?

Run it up the flagpole (and see if anyone salutes)

To try out an idea or plan, in order to gauge others' reactions to it. Like many a catchphrase, it has its origins in advertising, and specifically Madison Avenue in the 1950s, referring to testing ad campaigns or slogans before going ahead with them. The line is used by one of the jurors in Sidney Lumet's 1957 film *12 Angry Men*, and the American comedian Allan Sherman had this couplet in his 1963 parody of the Gilbert and Sullivan song 'When I Was a Lad': 'I said to the men in the dark grey suits, / "Let's run it up the flagpole and see who salutes."' There are variants, many of them parodies of the original phrase, such as 'Put it out and see if the cat eats it,' 'Throw it at the wall and see if it sticks,' or 'Put it on the train and see where it gets off,' though they are less popular. Even this expression is dying out, having long since lost its colour; it is, after all, only a verbose, and now hackneyed, way of saying 'Let's try it.' Like many expressions that originated in the advertising or PR industries, by the time it had gone into common usage, admen had long since stopped using it.

Run with (something), To

Not as in 'run with the pack', which means to go with the crowd or majority, nor even as in 'to run with the hare and hunt with the hounds', which means to support both sides in an argument or discussion, this comes once again from sport, as in 'to run with the ball'. (It was the act of a Victorian schoolboy in picking up a football and running with it that laid the foundations of the games of rugby and American football.) The phrase is now often used of ideas or plans: 'Okay, we'll take Steve's idea and run with it.' At most, it is just a jargonish way of saying 'develop' or even 'try out', and that is why its growing use is irritating: it is both contrived (since most of us are not hard–bitten sports coaches) and imprecise.

SAFE PAIR OF HANDS

Yet another sporting idiom, this one originating in Australia and applied originally to cricket, though it could just as easily be said of baseball, American football, or rugby, or any game where good catching is required either to further a play or to get an opponent out. It is used as a metaphor for someone honest, dependable, and who can be trusted to do an important job competently and without mistakes. However, the phrase often carries an air of faint praise, a slight sense that it may also mean 'sensible, unimaginative, slightly dull'. It is to be hoped that Stephen Hester, who replaced the disgraced

Fred (no longer Sir Fred) Goodwin as CEO of the Royal Bank of Scotland after it had to be bailed out to the tune of £45 billion (US $71 billion) of taxpayers' money – or £750 ($1,200) for every man, woman and child in the UK – is a safe pair of hands. It is best avoided if all you mean is 'not as incompetent/dishonest as the last person in that job'.

SELF-STARTER

This still means an electric (usually) device used to start an internal-combustion engine, but it has also come to mean someone who acts on his or her own initiative, who spots opportunities and who doesn't need to be told what to do before getting on with it. It is a staple of recruitment ads. Quite when the wonderful world of HR picked up on it isn't clear, but the earliest printed use dates from February 1960, in a job advertisement in *The Times*: '[the – male – applicant] Must be a self-starter but able to work within references given to him.' (It is interesting that the English used in HR-speak was atrocious even then, more than fifty years ago.) It has become tired to the point of meaninglessness in this sense, and is in any case a piece of wrong thinking: a self-starter is a device for starting something else, not itself.

SHAKEN, NOT STIRRED

A catchphrase that has become a cliché. Indeed, in 2005 it was ranked 90th out of 100 in the American Film Institute's list of best movie quotes (68 places lower than 'Bond. James Bond') – that's how overused it is. When, in his first James Bond novel, *Casino Royale* (1953), Ian Fleming described his hero's recipe for a dry martini of his own invention, he didn't actually mention stirring: 'Three measures of Gordon's, one of vodka, half of Kina Lillet [vermouth]. Shake it very well until it's ice cold, then add a thin slice of lemon peel.' It was not until *Dr No* (1958) that 007 uttered his second most famous line: 'Shaken and not stirred.' At the time, and especially in post–Second World War 'austerity' Britain, the phrase seemed the height of sophistication, and it has appeared in almost every Bond film since. Unfortunately, it has also been taken up by every cliché-monger there is, and notably journalists, many of whom are unable to resist its potential as a pun: 'Her performance left me shaken but not stirred,' a drama critic might write, while a sports correspondent might say that a coach's pep-talk had left a team shaken, but unfortunately not stirred. As Bond (Daniel Craig) says in the 2006 remake of *Casino Royale*, when a barman asks if he wants his martini shaken or stirred, 'Do I look like I give a damn?'

SING FROM THE SAME HYMN SHEET

This is a development of the older phrase 'To sing the same song [or 'tune']', for which the earliest printed reference, used in this metaphorical sense, is from a verse play by Robert Browning dating from 1846. Quite how the song became a hymn isn't clear, as hymn sheets – once handed out at the beginning of church services or prayer meetings either because the hymn to be sung wasn't in the hymn book, or because there were no hymn books – are rarely seen nowadays, perhaps because fewer and fewer people go to church. 'To sing from the same hymn sheet' means to present a united front, or, more broadly, to be sure that everyone is following the same procedure or plan, and its earliest use in this meaning seems to come from an article in *Newsweek* of April 1981. Its use has quickly become tiresome, not least because many who regularly employ it have probably never seen a hymn sheet in their lives. It runs the risk, too, of inadvertently causing infelicities that are at best risible, and at worst, downright idiotic, as for instance, 'We need to be certain that the atheist groups are all singing from the same hymn sheet.'

SIT DOWN (WITH *OR* ON)

A spectacularly fatuous way of suggesting or offering a meeting with someone or about something. It possibly has its origins in the use of 'sit down' to indicate more than simply the act of sitting, as in 'to sit down to a game of poker' or 'We never sit down thirteen at table', a usage that dates back to the sixteenth century, or in the sense, now mainly employed in America, of settling in a place or establishing oneself in a position – 'He sat down on a farm in Maryland.' Then again, it may come from the slightly later expression, now archaic, meaning to encamp in order to besiege a place, as in Sir Walter Scott's novel *Anne of Geierstein* (1829): 'The army of Burgundy sat down before Nancy, in a strong position' ('Nancy' in this case meaning the city in north-eastern France, rather than some hapless maiden). Whatever its origins, there can be no excuse for one (usually) seated person to say to another 'Let's sit down on this,' or 'I look forward to sitting down with you about this.' As one book on business–speak notes, 'It is jargon at its absolute rock–bottom silliest.'

SPEND MORE TIME WITH [MY/HIS/HER/YOUR] FAMILY, TO

This may mean what it says, but increasingly it is an overworked euphemism used to explain someone's reasons for withdrawing from public life, often following a scandal of some kind. In 2009 Tiger Woods announced that he was spending more time with his family. (Not with conspicuous success, for he and his wife divorced the following year.) But the phrase doesn't always refer to sexual scandal. In 1990 the British Employment Secretary Norman Fowler suspended his flourishing career to 'spend more time with my family'. Lord Fowler – as he became – a man of impeccable reputation, was indeed resigning for that reason and no other, and later returned to front–line politics. At the time, however, spending more time with the family implied catastrophe. The ensuing decade was a boom 'spending more time' time, especially for politicians, celebrities and sportsmen. And the phrase doesn't go away. In 2010 in *The*

New York Times, the American political satirist Stephen Colbert noted that the CEO of BP, Tony Hayward, had 'been resigned' in the wake of the *Deepwater Horizon* oil-slick disaster. 'He's looking forward to spending more time saying insensitive things to his family' (*see also* **Better late than never; Consider one's position**).

SQUARE THE CIRCLE

The phrase has a fine pedigree, being first recorded in print in one of John Donne's sermons, dating from 1624, while Matthew Prior's poem *Alma* (1717) includes the lines: 'Circles to square, and Cubes to double, Would give a Man excessive Trouble.' The concept is much older, however, going back at least to the Greek geometer Hippocrates of Chios (*c.* 470–*c.* 410 BC; not the famous physician, Hippocrates of Kos, who died around 370 BC). It refers to the problem in geometry – known as 'quadrature' – of producing a square of exactly the area of a given circle using a compass and straight-edge. Eventually, in the nineteenth century, it was proved that this is in fact impossible, for complex mathematical reasons beyond the scope of this book. By then, however, the expression had come to be used metaphorically to mean any impossible task. Increasingly, though, it has come to be used to mean anything that may be too difficult or too costly or too wasteful of time and other resources, rather than something that literally cannot be done. As a result, if someone is said to have squared the circle, it is now usually because he or she has found a workable solution to what had seemed an intractable problem. (It may also account for another piece of businessman's cant: 'A problem without a solution is not a problem.' Which is probably true enough, but deeply irritating none the less.)

STATE-OF-THE-ART

As a noun phrase, this first appeared in print, in an American photographic annual, in 1889 as 'status of the art', and as 'state of the art' in 1910. It means the current or latest stage of development in a particular technological or practical field, and its use as an adjective dates from 1955, in an article on aeronautics. In that form it has become tired from overuse, often inappropriately; a 'state-of-the-art camera' makes some sense to a listener (the phrase is commonly applied to cameras, computers, cell phones, 'portable media players' and similar devices, as well as being a favourite of the defence industry), but 'a state-of-the-art kitchen' implies something like a science lab, rather than a kitchen that happens to have a few up-to-date gadgets, which is usually what is meant. As long ago as 1988, a correspondent to *The New York Times* was complaining of a sign in a hotel in Dallas, Texas, that promised 'state-of-the-art room service', adding: '(Translation: cold, breathtakingly overpriced food arrives in just 75 minutes, instead of an hour and a quarter).' *See also* **Cutting edge**.

STUFF [OR SH*T] HAPPENS

US slang, originally as 'sh*t happens', of self-evident meaning, but often with overtones of a kind of fatalistic or resigned acceptance of whatever may occur. According to the *OED*, it first appeared in print in 1983, and by the 1990s was in regular use in newspapers on both sides of the Atlantic. Its slightly more euphemistic version gained currency when, in April 2003, the then US Secretary of Defense, Donald Rumsfeld, replied, in answer to questions about widespread looting in Baghdad: 'Stuff happens and it's untidy, and freedom's untidy, and free people are free to make mistakes and commit crimes and do bad things.' It is probably this that led to its becoming clichéd, increasingly used to mean 'Bad things happen sometimes,' but as a pure statement of fact, and no longer with the implication that it is something one has to accept. There is a resonance to the words when expressed by black American film-maker Spike Lee, talking of racism in the US: 'That sh★t happens every day.' Elsewhere, away from the streets – anachronistic.

SYNERGY

A word originally from Greek by way of Latin, meaning 'joint working, cooperation'; it also has a scientific meaning, in reference to the combined or related actions of groups of organs, and hence by extension to other fields such as mental health and pharmacology. Unfortunately, in the world of business, especially, it is now often used to mean the result of the cooperation, rather than the effort itself. The first reference in print, in this sense, dates from 1957, in a book called *Personality and Motivation* by the British–American psychologist R. B. Cattell, but by 1965 H. I. Ansoff was writing in his *Corporate Strategy* that 'synergy . . . is frequently described as the "2 + 2 = 5" effect to denote the fact that the firm seeks a product–market posture with a combined performance that is greater than the sum of its parts,' which is a bit less easy to grasp than 'joint working' or 'cooperation'. John Rentoul, in his *The Banned List: A Manifesto Against Jargon and Cliché* suggests that synergy and synergism should never be used except in writing about pharmacology or physiology. That the word is meaningless to most people, and incomprehensible to many, suggests that he is absolutely right.

TAKE A RAIN CHECK

An informal American expression, used properly when declining an invitation but expressing the hope that there will be another time – in other words, seeking a postponement. It comes from baseball, when, if a game was rained off, disappointed spectators were issued with rain checks (British 'cheques'), offering either a refund on their tickets or free admission at a later date. (It also came to mean a ticket that allowed one to order something not yet available, allowing one to collect it when it became so.) The first printed reference dates from May 1884, when the *St Louis Post-Dispatch* reported that several games had had to be abandoned because of rain, the audience receiving rain checks. As a phrase, it has therefore had a good run; however, it is now increasingly used simply to decline an invitation, without expressing any wish to attend on another occasion: 'You coming to Laura's wedding?' 'No, I think I'll take a rain check.' Its use in this sense makes the phrase pointless (it being at least a reasonable assumption that Laura will only get married once), and is best avoided.

TAKE IT TO THE NEXT LEVEL

According to one US-based website, this is 'MBA jargon', the sort of language favoured by those who hold (or are studying for) the Master of Business Management degree – in other words, management, business and consulting jargon. Little more than a roundabout way of saying 'improve' or, sometimes, 'expand', the phrase was spreading by the mid-1980s. Thus Donald M. Kendall, CEO of Pepsico (1971–86), talking to *The New York Times* about the State University of New York's Summerfare arts festival, which the drinks giant was then sponsoring, explained how he hoped the festival's new director was going to 'take us to the next level'. Why couldn't the latter just make Summerfare better, or broader in outlook, or livelier, or more 'accessible', or whatever else it was that Kendall meant? The phrase is often used by actors of their performances, with equal imprecision. But people who regularly use jargon clearly like the expression, perhaps because it makes it sound as though something rather mysterious and wonderful is being put in hand. But actually, it's pretty much meaningless verbiage, and as such can be dispensed with.

TAKE OUT
(*AS IN* 'TAKE OUT THE OPPOSITION')

Originally (in this sense, at least) a euphemism meaning to kill, assassinate, murder, obliterate or otherwise destroy, in which sense it goes back to the late 1930s, perhaps the earliest appearance in print being in Raymond Chandler's *The Big Sleep* (1939). Private eye Philip Marlowe, discussing the fate of a blackmailer with his client General Sternwood, has this line: '"I'll take him out," I said, "he'll think a bridge fell on him."' The term achieved prominence over the last thirty years, when state and military bureaucracies realized that the words 'killing' and 'destruction' could be bad box-office, PR-wise. The American TV 'evangelist' Pat Robertson's use of the term in 2005 was presumably to add a special I-play-with-the-big-boys *frisson* to his words. Musing on Venezuela's President Hugo Chávez during his TV show on the Christian Broadcasting Network, Robertson observed that the time had come to exercise 'the ability to take him out'. The evangelist, having momentarily forgotten the sixth Commandment – loosely, 'Thou shalt not take out' – subsequently apologized. Not so Barack Obama, who, running for the presidency, proclaimed 'We must take out Osama bin Laden.' And, in 2011, ordered the operation that did exactly that. The term, which has a certain gangsterish robustness, has become clichéd mainly because it is now often diluted to mean to obstruct or stop, as in 'We've got to take out their running backs' or 'Our new TV ad campaign is going to take out the opposition.'

THINK OUTSIDE THE BOX

Do get back in the box, Smith.

Another clichéd phrase from the world of business management. Like **Blue-sky thinking**, it advocates allowing the imagination to run free. The expression came into use some time during the second half of the twentieth century, an early appearance in print being in *Aviation Week & Space Technology* of July 1975: 'We must step back and see if the solutions to our problems lie outside the box.' The box is not, as you might expect, a metaphor for the narrow, confined space of conventional thought, but is believed to be based on an early-twentieth-century brainteaser, the nine-dot puzzle. There are nine dots on a piece of paper, drawn three by three to form a square grid. The challenge is to connect the dots with just four straight, continuous lines, without lifting the pencil from the paper. The trick is to allow some of the lines to extend *outside* the box. The drawback is that knowing you have to think outside the box does not supply the solution to the puzzle. After all, as you sit in a **brainstorming** session, your outside-the-box creative thinking could include cooking up an excuse not to visit the in-laws, or dreaming up a plausible reason for the failure of your financial forecasts, or compiling a mental birthday-present wish list . . .

THOUGHT SHOWER *SEE* BRAINSTORMING

Tick [*US:* Check] all the boxes, To

The satisfactory completion of a checklist of requirements. Ticking or checking boxes apparently began its invasion of the language in the mid-1990s, although the word 'checklist' itself originated in 1850s America. The media applies this sure-fire method of selection to everything from films and footballers to restaurants and motor cars, and on to profound and unknowable mysteries of the universe. And cattle: 'Simmental cows and Simmental cross cows really do tick all the boxes,' a farmer is quoted on the Scottish Farmer website, a delightful image. Consider: 'The Bentley Continental GTC ticks all the right boxes,' trumpets one online review of the car in question. Really? What about the boxes marked 'cheap' (a tad shy of £150,000/$237,000), 'economical' (6-litre engine returning an average 17.5mpg), 'green' (CO_2 rating: 618g/mile), 'sensible' (top speed 195mph/0–60mph 4.5 seconds)? So in the end it comes down to whose boxes, and who's doing the ticking. Which is reason enough not to use this overdone catchphrase – unless you're actually completing a checklist. A related expression, '[something or someone] ticks/doesn't tick my box' (and variants) is a colourful way of saying 'We hit/didn't hit it off,' or similar, but is best used sparingly.

TO TELL THE TRUTH/TO BE HONEST

Filler words only. No one would say 'To be dishonest, I think your speech was received really well . . .' or 'To tell an untruth, I don't think your bum looks big in that.' If anything, the impression this phrase might give is that the speaker is habitually dishonest. Its close cousin, 'To be perfectly honest', should ring even more alarm bells in a listener's brain.

TRANSPARENCY

A buzzword, in that it is currently fashionable, but often a weaselly one, and never more so than when deployed by governments or politicians or corporations to mean 'open to public scrutiny'. Because in normal usage the adjective 'transparent' often means 'open', 'candid', 'frank', it is a useful ally to anyone with something to hide, while at the same time giving the impression of being entirely sincere, honest and straightforward. The non-governmental organization Transparency International, based in Berlin, monitors and publishes details of corporate and political corruption, and has offices in some seventy countries. That it was established in 1993, and is still beavering away nearly twenty years later, probably says all there is to say about the true nature of 'transparency'. As an example, and despite all sorts of assurances, we are unlikely to see much transparency about bankers' bonuses, or government arms sales to possibly questionable regimes, any time soon, perhaps because the word seems to have nothing whatever to do with what ought to be its comrade-in-arms, 'accountability'. In short, whenever any organization – bank, government office, law firm, insurance company or similar – tells you that its processes are transparent, check and re-check the small print.

TRICKLE DOWN

'Trickle-down economics' or 'trickle-down theory' are terms associated with Reagan-era US politics, and refer to the principle that tax and other financial concessions accorded to the rich and to businesses will eventually trickle down to the poor, because of the overall benefits to the economy as a whole. The expression is actually said to have originated with the US actor and comedian Will Rogers who, during the Great Depression of the 1930s, said that 'money was all appropriated for the top in hopes that it would trickle down to the needy,' while *Webster's* dates its first appearance in print as an adjective to 1944. 'Trickle-down theory' was in use by 1954, and was decried by former President Lyndon B. Johnson in the early 1970s, so it was hardly very new when Republicans were trumpeting its benefits during Reagan's two terms in the 1980s. It was also criticized by the economist J. K. Galbraith (*see* **Affluent society**), while another leading American economist, Thomas Sowell, has stated that there is no such theory among economists. In other words, it is old hat and doesn't work – and much the same can be said of the now common usage of 'trickle down' to mean a general filtering downwards of money or ideas. Avoid it.

UNDER THE RADAR

In the Second World War, it was discovered that if an aircraft was flown low enough on the approach to its target it would be invisible to the enemy's radar, thus maintaining the element of surprise and wrong-footing anti-aircraft defences. Needless to say, flying an aircraft at anything from 50 to 200 feet above the ground requires a high degree of skill and – to use a cliché – nerves of steel.

However, from the 1950s 'radar' came to be used colloquially of a person's instincts, intuition and awareness, as in 'Her feminine radar was operating at full power.' Whether this influenced the adoption of 'under the radar' as a general term meaning 'undetected' or 'unnoticed', or even 'not standing out' or 'keeping a low profile', isn't clear, but thirty years later 'under the radar' – with its variants 'on/off the radar' – was well established among politicians, businessmen and journalists; one 1980s report about British MPs described them as 'getting under each other's radar'. By the twenty-first century Tupperware was reported as being mostly 'under the radar of design aficionados', a rather roundabout way of saying either that design aficionados simply don't notice the ubiquitous homeware, or that they despise it. Similarly, an overheard conversation between two thirty-something bankers in an expensive bar in London's City: 'Have you thought of buying a Mercedes CL-Class?' 'No. Can't say I have. **To be honest**, cheap cars don't really appear on my radar.' All of which seems rather far away from the courage and skill of pilots desperately trying to evade an enemy's radar defences . . .

UP TO SPEED

A term that originally meant that something has reached or is operating at full or working speed, as when, in a racing report from November 1879, *The New York Times* described a mare as looking 'decent and up to speed'. The phrase seems to have continued harmlessly in this literal meaning until the early 1970s, when it changed; the same paper reported in August 1974 that the phrase 'to bring [someone] up to speed' was sometimes used in the Watergate hearings to mean 'to brief'. It has now become a pest, meaning anything from 'familiar with' to 'experienced in' by way of 'completely informed about', as in 'Is he up to speed with the latest sales figures?' or 'I'm afraid I'm not up to speed with her latest boyfriends.' Given the choice of alternatives – 'conversant with', 'knowledgeable about', 'skilled in', 'abreast of', and so on – its continued use seems perverse.

USER-FRIENDLY

Another overworked term that we owe to the world of computing, its use dates from around 1977, while some sources say it was coined by an American software designer named Harlan Crowder as early as 1972. It means 'easy to use', 'designed with the needs of users in mind', and as such is convenient shorthand. The term has become a cliché through straying beyond its technological origins, probably because many people love to use technical expressions as an indication that they are hugely well informed, if not expert. As a result, the term is now not only overworked, but often used inappropriately. Describing a new cell phone as 'user-friendly' is helpful (at least, if it's true); describing a beef stew as 'user-friendly' is not only unhelpful, but plain silly. (*User Friendly* is also the title of J. D. Frazer's long-running webcomic about working life in a small Internet company, which first appeared in 1997.)

WAKE-UP CALL

A 1970s term for a telephone alarm call, it has been hijacked by politicians, sportsmen and commentators to mean something bad – or at least disappointing – that has happened, but which will serve to make sure the proper remedial action is taken. The term dates from the 1970s, but as 'wake-up service' first appeared in print, in a US newspaper, in 1946; its figurative use became commonplace in the 1980s. In the West, the most dramatic, as well as the most horrific, wake-up call of recent years was the terrorist assault on the USA in September 2001, which sent the country and its allies into swift action against international terrorism. It has become clichéd because it is so often used by politicians whose party has unexpectedly lost an election, and by sports commentators whenever a team loses unexpectedly to supposedly inferior opposition. It has its usefulness – as when referring to 9/11 – but if you just mean 'a warning' or 'a lesson', use those instead.

WHATEVER

A one-word get-out-clause that may combine two or more of insult, condescension, dismissiveness, uninterest, boredom, impatience, and 'I have lost the argument but I am damned if I will admit it.' The expression, which may derive from 'Whatever you say,' seems to have originated in the USA in the early 1970s, when it was used more to indicate acceptance, effectively saying to someone 'Do what you want, and I'll go along with it.' Its meaning changed slightly to indicate indifference, lack of concern or even boredom, in which sense it became established in Hollywood in the Reagan era in the 1980s, and moved speedily into the language of the sons and daughters of the Californian rich. It then spread, as a linguistic mutation of a communicable disease, via low-immunity vapid television into the vocabulary of the English-speaking West. Thus the *Village Voice* in July 1998: 'If someone came running to say he'd just seen Jesus preaching on the steps of the 72nd Street subway stop, most New Yorkers would reply, "Whatever".' It is a favourite with teenagers – yet another powerful reason for not employing it.

WINDOW OF OPPORTUNITY

A rather tired piece of political and business jargon that has its origins in astronomy, meteorology and rocket science, of all things. It probably came from the term 'launch window', used by the US space programme to indicate the optimal period in which a space vehicle must be launched; if that is missed, the launch has to wait for the next window. *Time* magazine first used 'window of opportunity', in reference to the Soviet Union, in an article in late 1979, and in 1984 a Republican Congressman, one Newton Leroy 'Newt' Gingrich, published a book entitled *Window of Opportunity: A Blueprint for the Future*, which probably helped to popularize the phrase. As with **pushing the envelope**, the expression is inoffensive when used in its original technical sense; too often, however, it is deployed as a long-winded way of saying 'chance', rather than to describe a brief period in which an opportunity must be seized. By extension, the irritatingly self-important habit in some professionally 'busy' people, of talking about having 'a window in their time frame', is not so much to be discouraged, as stamped on.

WIN-WIN (LOSE-LOSE, NO-WIN) SITUATION

It is a curious but interesting fact that the earliest printed references for 'no-win', 'win-win' and 'lose-lose' all date from the 1960s, the first two in 1962 and the last a year later. (Even more curiously, the citations for 'win-win' and 'lose-lose' both include the expression **zero-sum**, although that dates from the mid-1940s.) Originating in the USA, 'win-win' is really no more than a piece of self-congratulatory business-speak, and means only that all parties involved in some plan or enterprise benefit. Such an outcome is, in fact, extremely rare, and anyone planning on using the phrase should bear that in mind, for as often as not it is no more than an example of the wish being father to the thought.

With all (due) respect

With all **due** respect ...

Largely a euphemism for 'Please excuse me, but I am now going to contradict you,' the phrase uses 'due' in its sense of 'merited, appropriate, proper, right', the first printed reference to 'due respect' apparently dating from 1807. Today, useful substitutes for these words might easily include 'I am now patronizing you,' or, for those of a more timorous disposition, 'I am about to insult you – please do not hit me.' (There is also a subtext of 'I have not the least respect for you, but I am going through the motions.') Showing a greater respect for the niceties of international relations, Germany's Finance Minister, Wolfgang Schäuble, talking in 2010 of the policies of the US Federal Reserve, stated that, 'With all due respect, US policy is clueless.' As often as not the phrase conveys a kind of false humility, and if only for that reason is best avoided. It is also becoming increasingly long-winded, having gone from 'With respect' to 'With all respect' to 'With all due respect.' Whatever next? – 'With the greatest possible of all due respect'? Its sole merit, however, is that it is a tactful way of letting a senior, or at least someone with some power, know that you disagree with whatever he or she has said or is proposing. For this reason, it is much used by lawyers in court, and politicians in press interviews.

WITH THE BEST WILL IN THE WORLD

Apparently dating from the mid-1800s, the phrase indicates, in essence, that something is impossible, no matter how willing one is or how hard one tries. Unfortunately, it has acquired a certain weasel quality, especially in the mouths of politicians, who sometimes use it to describe something that is not going to be implemented or undertaken, with the subtext, 'Not a chance, but I do like to sound sincere.' The expression is overused anyway, often as a filler phrase with no greater meaning than that some scheme or proposed action isn't worth the time/effort/expense. Like **to tell the truth** or **to be honest**, it is a filler phrase, and anyone on the receiving end of it should consider whether or not the person using it is, in fact, being entirely – well, honest.

Work-life balance

Charmingly, the earliest printed reference to 'work life', in its original sense of 'working life', is a reference to live decoy ducks in a book about the English countryside published in the late 1940s. By 1977, however, the meaning had changed, so that 'work-life' or 'work/life' now usually refers to the relationship between one's job and one's personal life. (The first printed reference to its use in this sense was in a self-help book by an American management consultant, which probably says all that needs to be said.) A workaholic has a poor work-life balance; someone who works a few hours a week and spends the rest of the time at the races probably also has a poor work-life balance, but a great deal more fun. The balance exercises politicians and business people – and thus has been picked up by journalists, so that it is now often used to mean working a bit less, rather than establishing and maintaining a healthy and satisfying ratio between work and leisure. The phrase is a product of a world in which regular, long-term employment has given way to short-term employment and 'hot desks'. Beware of anyone who talks about his or her 'work-life balance'. What they usually mean is that they feel they are entitled to work fewer hours for the same – or higher – pay. In particular, beware of any manager who suggests you may want to consider your work-life balance, for this may well indicate that **downsizing** is in the air . . .

WORST-CASE (SCENARIO)

'Scenario' originally meant a sketch or outline for a play, a book, a film, and so on, and, by extension, the shooting script of a film. At some time in the early 1960s 'futurologists' began to use the word to mean a hypothetical future event, and especially a war, and the events that would follow from it. Before long, the word was being applied to any 'intended course of action' (*OED*), and has weakened still further until it now rarely means more than 'a circumstance, situation, scene, sequence of events, etc.' 'Worst-case' dates from roughly the same time, and seems to have its origins in scientific analysis; by the late 1970s the American journalist and novelist Robert Littell could write (in a spy novel, to be fair): 'Worst-case contingency planning is still the basis of scenario construction.' There is some excuse for that; none whatsoever for this sentence from an article in *Harper's Magazine* in January 1985: '[He] could spin off a royalty trust, perhaps sell the downstream operations . . . Such a move had been possible all along, but it was obviously the worse-case [*sic*] method of going about the task.' It is legitimate – just about – to use 'worst-case scenario' for, say, the planning of military operations in Afghanistan; it is tiresome, as well as long-winded, to use it to mean what might go wrong in everyday life or business.

WORST ENEMY, TO BE ONE'S OWN

The origins of the expression, according to *Allen's English Phrases*, go back to the sixteenth century, and by 1668, in his play *Mustapha,* Roger Boyle, first Earl of Orrery, was writing 'Thou mak'st my son his own worst Enemy.' Nowadays, own worst enemies – those allegedly bent on self-destruction, who discredit themselves – take so many different forms. Sarah Palin and English cricket are two singled out by the media but then, worst enemies are not always whom they appear to be. Four centuries on from Lord Orrery, the finest, and most quoted, use of the term remains that of Ernest Bevin, the British Foreign Secretary in the late 1940s. A colleague had suggested to him that Herbert Morrison, a fellow member of the Labour government (and grandfather of Lord [Peter] Mandelson) was 'his own worst enemy'. 'Not while I'm alive he ain't,' Bevin replied. The phrase is often used lazily, to mean someone who doesn't always get things right (or with whom the speaker disagrees), rather than someone likely to bring about his own downfall.

X IS THE NEW Y

This construction – called a snowclone for interesting reasons beyond the scope of this book – became enormously popular, in part for its potential for humour, but also for the snappy fashion-world ring it was born with, during the 1980s, and over-popular thereafter. The most usual 'Y' is black, the fashion world's favourite, the phrase being thought to originate with the designer Gianfranco Ferre, quoted in the *Los Angeles Times* (March 1983): 'Ferre says gray is the new black.' Ferre's words may have been inspired by press fashion reports such as *The New York Times*'s 'Colors are the new neutrals. Find a color you like and wear it with everything' (September 1979); it certainly led to a plethora of 'the new blacks' during the 1980s: 'There is a tremendous range to the color brown . . . It is the new black,' reported *The Washington Post* in March

1984. The marketing of electronic goods soon came up with 'small is the new big,' and further variations followed. The first decade of the twenty-first century is littered with 'X is the new Ys' of various degrees of absurdity: Microsoft on Zune's packaging in 2006: 'Brown is the new black is the new white'; 'Economizing is the new black' (*The New York Times*, May 2005);) 'Level is the new ahead' (Carol Bartz, CEO, Yahoo, 2009); and did it not occur to Ubank, a division of National Australia Bank when they came up with the slogan 'Saving is the new Spending' in 2009, that spending money means you have less money than you started with? In 2008 Lake Superior State University placed the expression on their 'Banished Words' list, declaring, 'The idea behind such comparisons was originally good, but we've all watched them spiral out of reasonable uses into ludicrous ones and it's now time to banish them from use.' Quite.

ZERO-SUM GAME

Neither a **win–win situation**, nor a lose–lose one, this is a state of affairs in which the gains of one side precisely equal the losses of the other. Chess, for instance, is not a zero-sum game, for it is possible for the winner to lose more pieces than the loser, yet still win. Dividing a cake into two unequal portions is a zero-sum game, for the person with the larger piece has gained by exactly the amount that the other person has lost. Like many clichés that have been adopted in business, politics and journalism, its meaning was once specific, in this case to game theory, a branch of mathematics and economics. It was coined – in its technical senses – by the great Hungarian-born American mathematician John von Neumann, and its earliest printed reference dates from 1944, in a book he wrote with the economist Oskar Morgenstern called *Theory of Games and Economic Behavior.* The phrase does not mean a game in which there are no winners, although that is increasingly how it is used – thus the *Handbook of Management Technology* in 1967: 'Everybody can win. Manufacturing is not a zero-sum game' – yet another example of the adage that technical language is best left to those who know how to use it. If you mean a game that has, or can have, no winners, then say so.

Select bibliography

BOOKS:

Allen, R., *Allen's Dictionary of English Phrases*, Penguin, 2006

American Heritage Dictionary of the English Language, The, fifth edition, Houghton Mifflin Harcourt, 2011

Ammer, C., *The Facts on File Dictionary of Clichés*, second edition, Checkmark Books, 2006

Brewer's Dictionary of Phrase and Fable, eighteenth edition, Chambers, 2010

Cambridge Idioms Dictionary, Cambridge University Press, 2006

Collins English Dictionary, tenth edition, HarperCollins, 2009

Kay, C., Roberts, J., Samuels, M. and Wotherspoon, I. (eds), *Historical Thesaurus of the Oxford English Dictionary*, Oxford University Press, 2009

Merriam-Webster's Collegiate Dictionary, eleventh edition, Merriam-Webster, 2003

New Oxford American Dictionary, The, second edition, Oxford University Press, 2005

Oxford Dictionary of Current English, fourth edition, Oxford University Press, 2006

Oxford English Dictionary, second edition (plus revisions), Oxford University Press, 1989, CD–ROM version 2009

Partridge, E., *A Dictionary of Slang and Unconventional English*, eighth edition, Routledge, 1984

Rentoul, J., *The Banned List: A Manifesto Against Jargon and Cliché*, Elliott & Thompson, 2011

Taggart, C., *Pushing the Envelope: Making Sense Out of Business Jargon*, Michael O'Mara Books, 2011

ONLINE:

The Business Dictionary: www.businessdictionary.com

Dictionary.com: dictionary.reference.com/

MBA Jargon Watch: www.johnsmurf.com/jargon

The Phrase Finder: www.phrases.org.uk

Urban Dictionary: www.urbandictionary.com/